Jung's Struggle with Freud

Jung's Struggle with Freud

George B. Hogenson

Revised Edition

Chiron Publications
Wilmette, Illinois

Originally published in 1983 by University of Notre Dame Press, Notre Dame, Indiana.

Library of Congress Catalog Card Number: 93-39285

Printed in the United States of America.
Cover design by Michael Barron

Library of Congress Cataloging-in-Publication Data:

Hogenson, George B.
    Jung's struggle with Freud / George B. Hogenson. — Rev. ed.
        p.   cm.
    Includes bibliographical references and index.
    ISBN 0-933029-81-0 : $14.95
        1. Jung, C. G. (Carl Gustav), 1875–1961 — Adversaries. 2. Freud,
    Sigmund, 1856–1939 — Adversaries. 3. Psychoanalysis — History.
    4. Psychoanalysts — Biography. I. Title.
    BF109.J8H64   1994
    150.19'54 — dc20   93-39285
                                                                                    CIP

    ISBN 0-933029-81-0

Cover: "Fossil: A Bird and a Flower" by Kunihiro Amano

*To the memory
of my
mother
and
father*

Contents

Preface

Ten years after *Jung's Struggle with Freud* originally went to press, its reprinting by Chiron Publications provides a rare opportunity for reflection on the continuing problem of the relationship the book set out to examine. A number of other books have appeared since 1983 that deal wholly or in part with the relationship between Freud and Jung. New materials continue to illuminate the more obscure aspects of the relationship, and new interpretations of various aspects are being developed. This is important work, for, as I remarked in the original preface to this book, one of the great lapses in the scholarly appraisal of Freud's achievement has been the failure to understand the role played by Jung in Freud's life and thought, not only during the years of their association but afterwards as well. I am increasingly convinced that much of the work done by Freud after the break with Jung, in particular the *Papers on Metapsychology*, was an attempt to respond to the alternative interpretation of the unconscious that Jung proposed. This point of view is important for understanding the argument of this book.

Both the history and the theory of psychoanalysis present problems for the interpreter, not the least because psychoanalysis is itself a theory of interpretation. Indeed, the central argument of *Jung's Struggle with Freud* is that Freud's system presents a unique theory of interpretation in that once one engages the theory it is almost impossible to step back out of its constraints and assess the phenomena independently. This characteristic of Freud's system leads to the thematic problem of the book, Freud's claim to authority in the realm of the psyche. Some readers have found this theme problematic: why shouldn't Freud claim authority in psychoanalysis? He was the founder after all, and Jung certainly did not distinguish himself in generosity toward Freud. Wasn't Freud perfectly correct to say that Jung was simply following the crowd that wanted to reject the immorality of Freud's vision of the unconscious? Fastidious Victorian sensibilities are hardly the basis for the scientific investigation of our inmost secrets. This argument takes us to the heart of the problem of interpretation in depth psychology: What exactly do we know about the unconscious, and how do we know it?

Human beings think in spatial and temporal terms. Notwithstanding the extraordinary formalism of quantum mechanical theory in physics, which conceives of the fundamental constituents of matter in purely mathematical terms, we still think of the atom and its parts along the lines of a small solar system. Similarly, in depth psychology, we invariably think of the unconscious along the lines Freud suggested in his early topographic model. The unconscious is a place in psychical space. One still hears references to the "subconscious" as if the psyche had structure like a building, a part of which was down below. Most of the metaphors used by both Freud and Jung reinforce this mental image. For Freud, the unconscious is a dark cellar full of discarded and somewhat damp artifacts cast off by the consciousness up above. But to understand the central conflict between Freud and Jung, as I try to outline it in this book, we have to grasp the fact that the unconscious is very much a mystery even to its most insightful investigators.

To add another spatial metaphor, the unconscious is a black box, an unknown set of mechanisms. A person has experiences, perhaps beginning prenatally, and then, as an adult, comes to the therapist with some behavioral complaint. In between, the depth psychologist maintains, some process takes place within the unconscious that converts the experience into the behavioral response. The problem for depth psychological theory, what Freud called metapsychology, is to define what mechanisms inside the black box are operating on the experiences of the individual such that the manifest behavior will be the outcome.

Jacques Lacan has given us the most lapidary formulation of what the unconscious is like when he states that the unconscious is structured like a language. In making this statement he claims to be closely following Freud, although influence comes at least as much from the linguist Ferdinand de Saussure, and the anthropologist

Claude Lévi-Strauss. But by saying that the unconscious is structured like a language, Lacan is saying that the activities of the psyche follow the rules of linguistic transformation. Experience is coded, for Lacan, in the same way that we form metaphors or figures of speech. Lacan is useful here because his model is so simple, regardless of the contortions he puts it through as he develops its implications. The point, however, is that it remains a conjecture passed off as a fully knowable structure.

The problem is that we have never really seen the unconscious, any more than we have seen a subatomic particle or, for that matter, a gene. What we see are effects from which we derive hypotheses that are more or less testable, insofar as they predict further effects or, in the case of the hermeneutical sciences such as psychoanalysis, provide more or less powerful interpretations of past events.

This state of affairs presented a problem for both Freud and Jung, because they were both committed to the ideals of empirical science. Jung's critics typically overlook that, already before he met Freud, he enjoyed international recognition as an experimental psychologist for his work on the word association test. Not only had he designed and built instruments that at last allowed refined measurement of associational phenomena, he had also developed the first fully convincing interpretations of those phenomena. It was his theorizing about why some people had delayed responses to some stimulus words that gave rise to the term *complex*, which eventually came to dominate psychoanalysis when it was joined to Freud's understanding of the drama of Oedipus. Jung's writings on the word association test also provided the occasion for his first encounter with Freud, because Jung thought he had finally found some experimental evidence that supported Freud's theory of repression. Freud's early enthusiasm for Jung was also influenced by the implications of this experimental evidence. But the word association test haunts the relationship between Freud and Jung. I now believe it was Jung's work with the test, as much as anything else, that caused his initial, and continuing, skepticism about Freud's insistence that sexuality was the univocal source of psychic disturbance. The associative patterns that were evident in the responses of test subjects were simply too various to be reduced to a single causal factor, while at the same time they clearly showed that a process of psychic distortion was at work. Again, it was Jung's lectures at Fordham University in 1912, given on the occasion of his receiving an honorary doctorate recognizing his research on word association, that led Freud to conclude that Jung had finally rejected psychoanalysis. In 1935 there was an almost comic quality to Jung's Tavistock lectures where he clearly wanted to discuss the empirical findings of the word association test while his audience, by then convinced of the popular notion that Jung was some sort of mystical guru, only wanted to discuss every possible form of esoterica. Much more needs to be said about Jung and the word association test before we are able to understand fully the foundations of his theory of the psyche, including his position on archetypes, which derives from this earlier work.

The word association test was important to Freud because it held out the hope of experimental tests for his theory. But he himself had taken a different investigative tack before his association with Jung. Between roughly 1895 and 1900 Freud worked through what came to be known as his self-analysis. This experience is critical to understanding the argument of *Jung's Struggle with Freud*, for it is my contention that Freud's claim is that in the self-analysis he was able to open the black box of the unconscious and examine its parts. What I have said up to this point concerning the scientific problem of investigating the unconscious is intended to draw into stark relief the significance of this claim. To get psychoanalysis, properly so called, up and running, Freud questioned his own life concerning the mechanisms at work in converting experiences into meanings and behaviors. This was a daring move on Freud's part, but from it came the essentials of his system, not only the theory of repression but most importantly the interpretation of the Oedipus complex and the theory of the sexual etiology of the neuroses.

The problem with this approach, however, is that it cannot be replicated. For all we know, Freud's unconscious worked exactly the way he said it did. But there is no way to test this hypothesis. Additionally, as I argue in this study of the relationship, Freud constructed an interpretation that makes it difficult, if not impossible, to move from within his system back to a direct experience of the unconscious. In other words, Freud claims to have had a direct encounter with the unconscious and then sets things up in such a way that the experiment cannot be replicated if one wants to stay within the frame of psychoanalysis. Precisely how Freud accomplishes this restrictive move, and its impact on and implications for Jung, forms the thematic core of the book.

There is another neglected aspect to the development of psycho-analysis in the historical and philosophical literature: most writers do not give nearly enough attention to the nature of the clinical experience associated with doing psychotherapy. Freud in particular is treated almost as if he was conducting chemical experiments in a laboratory. In fact, the clinician is constantly surrounded by inexplicable phenomena that are usually subsumed under the categories of transference and countertransference. But these broad categories do little to capture the feelings of dislocation and confusion, sometimes of sheer terror, that arise in the consulting room. Even today, therapists rarely discuss these experiences in the literature, and the non-clinical commentators seem to have no awareness that they exist. But Freud, and the other early pioneers in the field, must have constantly confronted similar experiences. Much is made of Joseph Breuer's retreat from the erotic transference of Anna O, as if the problem was simply one of moral conflict. But I suspect that Breuer was experiencing powerful countertransferences that might now be used for purposes of interpretation but were to him a matter of inexplicable emotional—and probably physiological—stimulation. These phenomena of clinical experience need to be more tightly integrated into our reconstruction of the early history of psychoanalysis because one can view much of the development of theory as a means of getting control over those phenomena. We must realize that the phenomena the early investigators encountered were probably extremely disorienting, even frightening, and totally uninterpreted. Theory then becomes a buffer against the experiences as much as it becomes a way of understanding them. Depth psychological theories are defense mechanisms.

There is no question that Freud's theoretical system is a dominant element in contemporary discourse, but it is vital to understand the deep structure of that system and its implications for our thinking and actions. If I am correct, and the relationship between Freud and Jung is truly critical for understanding either man, we must ask what we can learn from the relationship concerning the historical structure of the twentieth century. Sigmund Freud wrote *The Interpretation of Dreams* in 1899 but had the publisher date the book 1900 because he believed it would define the new century. He was not far wrong. C. G. Jung, at the age of 25, was one of the first readers of Freud's masterpiece. For both men the role of myth took on paramount importance for their theories of the psyche. Indeed, in this book I argue that a powerful form of self-mythologizing is at work in their relationship. Myth, of course, was supposedly banished by the Enlightenment, and the orthodox reading of Freud is that he continues the Enlightenment process of overcoming myth. To claim, as I do, that he was engaged in building a very powerful and intricate myth is to take a heterodox point of view. And if I am correct, then the work of myth is ongoing in our time, and Freud's epochal book is part of that process.

Jung did not think human beings could live without myth. This insight was the theme of his own encounter with the unconscious discussed in *Jung's Struggle with Freud*, and it became the theme of his life work. It seems to me that Jung's theory of myth is, in the end, far more sophisticated than Freud's. In Jung's approach to myth we find an argument for what contemporary psychological research would call cognitive structures. Myth, on this reading, is one important way, if not the important way, in which human beings comprehend the world around them. To inhabit the world by recourse to myth — and related behaviors such as ritual — is to be human. Myth, Jung says, is part of the organism. To deny its importance is to seek a disembodied idealization of the mind like that first posited at the beginning of the Enlightenment in the seventeenth century. The form of this ideal is Descartes's cogito or Leibniz's monad, neither of which have any spatial, bodily dimension, although both are capable of essentially godlike rationality.

The other side of this point of view is that some idealized rationality alone cannot constrain the working of myth in our lives and in our institutions. Rationality, which, when applied to human behavior, becomes modern economics and its derivatives, is unquestionably also a means for providing cognitive structure, and it has certainly been used by human beings to comprehend their world all along. The problem of the Enlightenment apotheosis of rationality is that it seeks to drive out all other forms of world comprehension. Jung's argument is that such an attempt to get rid of myth, to demythologize, is an invitation to neurosis, if not to psychosis. This is where Jung is directly at variance with Freud, at least at the level of theory. Freud's theory sees the continuing presence of myth as indicative of a fundamental, indeed primordial, psychopathology. Jung sees the well-ordered but continued presence of myth as an indication of psychological health. Attempts to eliminate myth from our lives are, then, invitations to psychopathology. In the end, Jung would say, myth cannot be eliminated, and so one has to learn to live with it. Again, contrary to many of Jung's critics, this is emphatically not an argument for Romanticism. If anything, it is again a highly empirical, observational position that draws on ethological and cybernetic evidence concerning the self-regulation of the organism. What differentiates Jung is that he is willing to include all forms of human experience in his investigations. He does not count anything out as irrational or as an illusion. If a particular way of interacting with the world has been around for a long time, as myth has been, it is probably there for a reason. To say that myth or religion are forms of pathology is equivalent to saying parallax vision is a form of pathology. What is pathological, Jung would say, is loosing sight in one eye. Then you cannot register depth, and you will have difficulty dealing with the world.

The twentieth century is a study in such imbalances. In Nazi Germany myth went wild and threatened to take over. Anyone who thinks that true happiness lies in a romantic return to the world of myth alone is playing at the edge of an abyss. By contrast, much of the theorizing that drove the nuclear arms race can be seen as an instance of rationality gone wild. The problem in both cases is that the blind eye continues to work its will. In the case of the Nazis, it was not so much the myth of Aryan superiority that led to disaster, but rather the power of instrumental reason, coupled to industrial organization, neither of which had any place in the romantic nativism of the myth, that allowed the Holocaust of the Jews and other acts of destruction to reach the scale they did. Again, in contrast, the mythic quality of the construction of the other as diabolical enemy has been the unspoken driving force behind much of the highly rationalized arms race since 1945.

Both Freud and Jung proposed ways to regulate the working of myth in the lives of human beings. Taken as means of understanding modernity, both thinkers provide powerful insights that cannot be ignored. In the end, I believe Jung's system has more potential for providing the deep level of understanding needed to grasp how myth works in our individual and collective lives. And Freud's understanding of the development of the individual psyche provides the basis for other important work, as can be seen in the so-called neo- or post Freudian theories of Klein, Winnicott, and Kohut.

In their own struggle, however, I see Jung and Freud playing out important aspects of the problem of myth in human life. This is the point of my brief comment on anti-Semitism in chapter one of *Jung's Struggle with Freud*. In the end, I think Jung found a better way out of the problem, although he may at times have failed to live up to the potential of his insights in his actual life. Freud, let it be said, was not always the paragon of rationality he wanted to be, either.

By way of concluding this preface, a brief overview of the book itself may be helpful to the reader. Chapter one introduces the problem of authority. To do this I highlight an incident that took place on a crossing to America undertaken by Jung and Freud in 1909. In his recollection of this incident, Jung thematizes Freud's need for authority and his own rejection of Freud's claim. The incident is important for this thematic quality. It provides a window on the problem of law and anti-law (antinomianism) that will play a role later in the book.

Chapter two takes up the problem of myth. Here I argue that two critical texts, Jung's doctoral dissertation and Freud's book on Leonardo da Vinci provide basic insights into the mythic patterns at work in the self-understanding of each man. In this chapter, I introduce a term that helps to organize the rest of the book: *metabiography*. In essence, the notion of metabiography holds that certain structural characteristics of a life narrative, a biography, can become normative for understanding the nature of biography in general. Jung and Freud start their association with quite different understandings of the meaning of fundamental experiences in their respective lives, and these differences become the basis for a metabiographical conflict as each attempts to demonstrate that his life narrative truly provides the categories for biographical understanding in general.

Chapter three continues the theme of metabiography by, examining two texts written near the end of their association: Jung's *Symbols and Transformations of Libido* and Freud's *Totem and Taboo*. By this point in their association both Freud and Jung understood that the end of their relationship was imminent, and the two texts can also be read as a commentary on the break.

Chapter four reviews Freud's theory of repression, which, at the end of the discussion of *Totem and Taboo*, emerged as the critical element in his theory of the psyche. At this point, the discussion turns to the problem of the primordial constitution of the psyche. This is important for understanding the mythic quality of both Freud's and Jung's theories. A serious problem confronts the founders of depth psychology in that they must give an account of how and why there is an unconscious in the first place. But the account given, particularly in the case of Freud, is itself mythical. It has all the qualities of a creation myth and I therefore refer to it, and its analogue in Jung's theory, as a cosmogony, a story about the origins of the world. It is also the case, however, that Freud and Jung are, at this late point in their relationship, trying to prove their points by acting them out. Thus, I must consider in some detail Freud's desire to die, directly in keeping with his myth of the primal horde developed in *Totem and Taboo*.

Chapter five takes us to the heart of the problem of authority in psychoanalysis. The argument here is that the drama of Oedipus, which Freud considered the linchpin of his system, is open to a variety of interpretations. Freud proposes one interpretation that, I argue, is constructed in such a way that Freudian psychoanalysis itself is confirmed in the interpretation. Let me emphasize that this is not simply because Freud's interpretation arises out of his system. Rather, the interpretation establishes the system and confirms Freud's unique claim to accurately understand and interpret the activities of the unconscious. Jung, on the other hand, proposes a different reading of Oedipus, leading to a prospective sense of personal development, which he attempted to act out after the break with Freud.

Chapter six argues that the problems raised in relation to Freud's theory of repression and the conflict of interpretations regarding the Oedipus drama come to rest on the understanding of time in relation to the unconscious. The key here is to ask in what direction do we look when we act out of the unconscious. For Freud, I argue, the point of view is always retrospective; for Jung it is prospective, toward the future.

Jung's prospective point of view leads to a discussion of projection in chapter seven. My reading of Jung leads to the conclusion that projection is the primordial and world constituting act of the psyche in his theory, just as repression is in Freud. Projection leads into a discussion of phantasy in Jung and a reading of his *Seven Sermons to the Dead* that marked the end of his own encounter with the unconscious, an encounter that corresponded in many respects to Freud's self-analysis.

Chapter eight is an overview of the argument of the book and attempts to show how the various pieces fit together.

In preparing this reprinting of *Jung's Struggle with Freud* I have resisted a wholesale revision of the book. I have attempted in a few places to provide a bit more clarity where a particular point of fact or argument seemed obscure. I have purposely retained one orthographic convention that has caused some confusion: The Standard Edition of the works of Freud renders the German "Phantasie" as "phantasy" while the Collected Works of Jung render it as "fantasy." All citations retain the spelling used in the translation. I, however, use "phantasy" throughout, because I believe it captures the deeper sense both Jung and Freud attached to the concept. Jung revised many of his early works in such a way that his reader could not distinguish ideas developed in 1912 from those developed in 1950. My argument in this book is unchanged. What seems most important is that this part of an ongoing dialogue with both Freud and Jung remain available to the general reader.

Acknowledgments

I owe a debt to many people for both the original version of this book and for its appearance in revised form. My friend and teacher, Rulon S. Wells, remains an inspiration to the entire project. Richard Allen, William Borden, Norman O. Brown, Robert Danly, Siobhan Drummond, Maurice Natanson, Kristin Pfefferkorn, Andrew Samuels, Carl Schorske, Nathan Schwartz-Salant, Catherine Shoupe, Murray Stein, Peter Swales, and Jennifer Widner all offered valuable advice at various stages in the writing of the book, either in its original or its revised versions. The staffs of the Beinecke Rare Book and Manuscript Library at Yale and the Francis A. Contway Library at Harvard provided invaluable assistance by allowing me access to their special collections dealing with C. G. Jung. Throughout the revision of the book, my wife Kate has consistently offered her good-humored love and encouragement, for which I am deeply grateful.

Abbreviations

CW   Jung, C. G., *Collected Works* (volume:paragraph)
FJL   McGuire, Wm., *The Freud/Jung Letters*
FP   Ricoeur, Paul, *Freud and Philosophy*
GR   Jonas, Hans, *The Gnostic Religion*
LP   Laplanche, J., *The Language of Psychoanalysis*
MDR   Jung, C. G., *Memories, Dreams, Reflections*
MR   Bachofen, J. J., *Myth, Religion and Mother Right*
PEY   Campbell, J., *Papers From the Eranos Yearbooks* (volume: page)
PR   Hegel, G. W. F., *Philosophy of Right*
PS   Hegel, G. W. F., *Phenomenology of Spirit*
SE   Freud, Sigmund, *Standard Edition* (volume: page)

One

Meaning and Authority

Freud had a dream. I would not think it right to air the problem it involved. I interpreted it as best I could, but added that a great deal more could be said about it if he would supply me with some additional details from his private life. Freud's response to these words was a curious look, a look of the utmost suspicion. Then he said, "But I cannot risk my authority." At that moment he lost it altogether. That sentence burned itself into my memory; and in it the end of our relationship was already foreshadowed. Freud was placing personal authority above truth. (MDR 158)

The Problem of Authority

This passage from C. G. Jung's memoirs records an event on a voyage to America, in 1909, marking the first truly international recognition of Freud's psychoanalytic theories. Freud and Jung had been invited to participate in the celebration of the twentieth anniversary of Clark University in Worchester, Massachusetts, and traveled there together with Sandor Ferenczi. The three men, joined in New York by Ernest Jones and A. A. Brill, were together virtually every day for seven weeks. They devoted their time in America to academic ceremony and discussions of Freud's theory of the sexual etiology of the neuroses. They became acquainted with eminent figures in the academic and medical communities. Both Freud and Jung met with William James.

But Jung's memory of the ocean passage focuses our attention on the central problem of this essay: What does it mean to lay claim to personal authority in a world where biography and autobiography have become thematic for an entire cultural discourse? How are we to comprehend authority in psychoanalysis? In Jung's recounting of the episode, the problem of authority begins as one of interpretation, in this case the interpretation of a dream tied to the complexities of Freud's familial relationships.[1] Jung claimed that interpretation required access to this biographical information; Freud refused to provide it. Should Freud have provided this information? Freud was senior to Jung by twenty years and was, after all, the founder of psychoanalysis. Freud's sense of his position within the still-young psychoanalytic community was unquestionably in keeping with the academic traditions of the time, which placed the authority of the master beyond question. Was Jung trying to overturn this tradition, a tradition within which he was himself already advancing?

A variety of conjectures are possible, but it nevertheless remains the case that if we put this exchange regarding authority in the mouth of any dreamer other than Freud himself, and judge it by the standards of Freud's own clinical theories, we would consider the dreamer to be indulging in a form of resistance. But I propose to show that this moment in Jung's struggle with Freud, when the master sets a prohibition on interpretation, on the employment of his own method for putting the question to the unconscious, is emblematic of the nature of authority in psychoanalysis. Here, I will argue, we witness one instance of a paradoxical dialectic of disclosure and foreclosure in relation to the unconscious that is at the heart of psychoanalysis. For Freud, the demand for disclosure and the right to foreclosure arise from his historically unique experience of the unconscious in his self-analysis.

But how does this claim become part of the controversy over interpretation and access to the unconscious in the personal struggle between these two men? Why does it not simply resolve itself into an academic controversy? To begin to answer these questions we must constantly remember that Freud's method of interpretation is ultimately defined by the universal significance of one act of self-understanding—Freud's own, in his self-analysis—for any possible subsequent act of self-understanding. Freud's self-analysis, in other words, makes a unique claim on all projects of self-understanding that come after it. And this claim, I will argue, is not the same as that made by investigators in other field's precisely because the basis for the claim rests on self-referential insights that cannot be separated from the person of the investigator. But the core of the problem lies not in self-analysis per se, but rather in the problematic of generalization from the individual to the universal. What, we will have to ask, is at stake when the life narrative of one individual—whether it is Freud or, as we will see, Jung following the break with Freud— becomes normative for the interpretation of other lives? What happens when method and insight link the individual and the universal?

Freud claimed that in his self-analysis he had discovered the fundamental structures and mechanisms that constituted the human psyche. The key to this system was the nature of the unconscious, to which the dream was the *via regia*, the Royal Way. The way was not clear, however. To find one's way to the unconscious, and to understand its structure, thus grasping the truth of Freud's theories, the truth seeker had to interpret the dream. Only one method would lead unerringly through the maze of deceptive images thrown up by the unconscious. That method was a hermeneutics of suspicion, to use Paul Ricoeur's phrase, which refused to accept the manifest meaning of the dream's representations and always sought to overcome resistance found on the way. This was the method Freud had taught to Jung. But now "Freud had a dream" that he refused to allow Jung, his close associate and chosen heir, to follow into the depths of the unconscious.

The Dramatic Moment

Philosophy has traditionally sought to transcend the particular individual in its quest for the universal forms of knowledge and being. Early in the nineteenth century, however, Søren Kierkegaard alerted philosophy to the problematic nature of this tradition and made a peculiar form of autobiography, his pseudonymous works, into material for thinking. Psychoanalysis is, in part, heir to this philosophical turn, and, as Jung sits with Freud in a ship's cabin, the actions of the two men become an existential performance of a system of thought. Philosophy emerged from just such a world where, in the drama of the Greek stage, the performance of an idea defined the terms of personal reference for the larger community. In our own century, it was Freud who first showed how the encounter of the individual observer with tragic drama, both on the stage and in one's own life, could be used to infer the structure and mechanics of the psyche.

3

This essay records the drama of the encounter of Freud with his disciple Jung, and it seeks to show just how it is that this encounter is itself a performance of an idea, the tragic drama of a failure of understanding. By thus fulfilling the existential demand that philosophy address the concrete individual, we will be drawn back to a point prior to philosophy, to the universality of tragic drama, from which philosophical reflection may begin.

The tragic drama of the Greeks was and is understandable because of prior knowledge and expectation in the audience. This prior knowledge and expectation depends, in turn, on the availability of mythic narratives or other familiar precursors of the dramatized action. This gives the drama a certain timeless quality in its ability to recover memory, but the performance of the drama disturbs these prejudgments of the action and leads to the emergence of a new understanding of the foundational myth itself. This process of understanding, and the emergence of ever new meanings distinguished by their timeliness, defines the essence of hermeneutics as a form of understanding.

But as the dramas themselves demonstrate, in the overcoming of a Creon, for example, it is precisely the emergence of a timely meaning, by way of interpretative understanding, that defeats the assertion of authority. Only when "concealment is overcome" (*Antigone*, line 1296) does authority give way to meaningful order. By claiming to follow just this process of unconcealment, Freud's program of psychoanalysis begins to reveal its own origins in a mythic impulse.

Freud dominates the interpretative discourse of our culture, and it is one of my objectives to show why this is the case. The first step in this process of domination is the annexation, by the prejudgments of psychoanalysis, of our deeply embedded comprehension of the role hermeneutical understanding plays in overcoming repression, whether it be in Antigone's quest for meaning or in the appeal to hermeneutics proper that marked, in the recovery and interpretation of the fundamental texts of Christianity, the Reformation's break with traditional clerical authority. By approaching the dramatic performance of Jung's struggle with Freud, however, the same hermeneutical process leads us to a disruption of this received meaning. The continuation of the interpretative process, applied now to an acting out of the central metaphor of psychoanalysis in the confrontation of father and son, leads us to a new understanding of Freud based on his renunciation of his own canons of method in favor of a claim to authority based on the foreclosure of interpretation. We will thus discover that one critical aspect of the Freudian myth is to vindicate power at the expense of meaning.

By becoming engaged in this reunderstanding of Freud's myth, we will become aware of another aspect of the problem of meaning in modernity. As creators of mythic systems, both Jung and Freud can be understood as cosmogonists. The struggle over the predefinition of biographical understanding is nothing less than a primordial struggle of world constitution. Given the notion that understanding is hermeneutical, an assumption Freud and Jung both accepted and shared with a prominent group of contemporary social scientists and philosophers, then possessing the right to define the prejudicial world, the dominant myth, is decisive for situating oneself in the vanguard of the culture. To an extraordinary degree Freud succeeded in his effort to constitute a dominant myth. Jung, however, did not fail in his own attempt but rather found himself compelled to exist, because of the success of Freud's undertaking, in the dark world of a counter-myth based on a Gnostic vocabulary that had served other advocates of the counter-tradition for centuries. Eventually, this allowed Jung to offer a profound interpretation of that tradition in the analysis of alchemy he undertook late in his life.

Authority, the Sacred, and Psychosis

The problem of interpretation and understanding, resting on a theory of myth, points us in the direction of the constitution of quasi-religious or sacred systems. At the same time, the appeal to the unconscious, as the foundation of the myth of both Freud's psychoanalysis and Jung's depth psychology, will eventually bring us into contact with forms of disturbed consciousness, particularly psychotic disturbance. This combination of the sacred and psychosis, at the heart of psychoanalysis, will lead us to a point where our interpretation will be forced to address the problematic that they both define: the loss and recovery of the world. The unification of all these elements in the origins of psychoanalysis will thereby bring this essay into contact with contemporary hermeneutical philosophy. The status of the sacred is a major issue for those philosophers who concern themselves with the nature of tradition and interpretation. Thus Heidegger, Gadamer, and Ricoeur all seek, by means of hermeneutics, to define the place of the sacred in the history of thought.

It is Ricoeur's concern for a recovery of the sacred through hermeneutics that draws him into his extraordinary philosophical encounter with Freud. Notwithstanding the power of this interpretation, I believe Ricoeur has misconstrued Freud insofar as he has failed to deal with the confrontation between Freud and Jung. It is in the interpretation of this confrontation that we come to see Freud as engaged in an act of sacralization that focuses on his own encounter with, and interpretation of, the unconscious, during his self-analysis. Jung, on the other hand, seeks an interpretation that will allow him to escape from what he sees as Freud's dogmatic representation of the numinous in the form of a psychology of the unconscious.

As this argument develops, the crisis surrounding Freud's authority, which appears at first to be nothing more that an inappropriate intrusion of the student upon the master, unexpectedly turns out to rest on the problem of the constitution of a system of symbols for our age. As the argument progresses, the fact that the Jung/Freud dispute focuses on myth will show that in psychoanalysis authority depends upon an interpretation of a person's self-consciousness in relation to time, for which the deployment of a system of time-transcending symbols is essential. The horizon of the mythic is time, to paraphrase Heidegger, in that a myth and its symbols organize our interpretative understanding of both past and future. A myth is a system of symbols oriented to the comprehension of time. But myths not only serve as organizing principles for contemplation; they also give rise to action that shapes the comprehension of time.

Freud and Jung derive their respective myths from a combination of deep personal experience with the unconscious and highly idiosyncratic investigations of the religious traditions of the world. To work out the significance of myth in their lives, we will have to examine these unusual avenues of investigation. It is also essential, however, to keep in mind the existential drama of Jung's recollection of the ocean passage. The need for a few details from Freud's private life points us to an area where biography and mythology become implicated in one another. This is where thought and action are joined.

The Relationship and Its Interpretation

As a first step in exploring the confrontation between Jung and Freud, attention will concentrate on the years of their collaboration, that is, between 1906 and 1913, with excursions into the years immediately before that time and into the working out, by both men, of their reactions to the break. This period has been selected for the obvious reason that the interaction between the two men was most prominent during the time they were with one another. Beyond that, I will show that it is out of this collaboration that the essential terms for understanding their future development arise. Thus the essay deals with a period of about twenty years, from Jung's writing of his dissertation in 1902 to his publication in 1920 of *Psychological Types*, a work in which he sought to explain why psychoanalysis should break down into schools such as those of Freud, Adler, and his own. Another reason for concentrating on this period is the existence of the remarkable collection of letters that passed between Freud and Jung. One finds there an almost unlimited field of nuance and subtlety. It is in this exchange of letters, rather than in any of their other writings, whether they be *The Interpretation of Dreams* or *Memories, Dreams, Reflections*, that the two genuinely reveal themselves.

The correspondence began in April 1906, when Freud wrote to Jung to thank him for a copy of his latest publication on word association. It continued until April 1914, when Jung withdrew as president of the International Psychoanalytic Association. In 1923 Jung wrote to Freud to refer a patient to him, but otherwise there was no contact after the break. In 1906, however, Jung was emerging as a strong defender of Freud's theories within the medical community. He was, nevertheless, an equivocal advocate, and in a letter to Freud in October 1906 he made it clear that he did not consider the genesis of hysteria to be exclusively sexual (FJL 5). Freud's attitude to Jung's reservations, in this instance and for some time to come, was indulgent. The indulgence first took the form of expecting Jung shortly to come around to Freud's point of view by gaining greater psychoanalytic experience. Later it became increasingly colored by a psychoanalytic interpretation that saw Jung's objections as classic expressions of resistance, while Jung saw them as the result of empirical observation. This points to an early and persistent conflict between the two men that, on one level, reflects their distinct empirical experiences. The correspondence can be read, largely, as a dispute over what kinds of data are admissible in the formulation of psychoanalytic theory.[2]

The general tendency in the literature of psychoanalysis is to ignore the relationship altogether or to see in the relationship the vindication of one or the other theories developed in the wake of the break in relations. Thus the Freudians see Jung in classical oedipal terms, desiring to supplant the father, and Jungians see Freud as a precursor to Jung's more elaborate psychology. This situation is complicated by the tendency of commentators in both camps to produce secondary literature that is all too often hagiographic in nature and therefore of limited usefulness. In this study, consequently, sparing use is made of the secondary materials on the lives of Jung and Freud. This also serves a systematic objective in that the focus here is on those aspects of their lives that are philosophically significant, aspects that are well represented in their respective published works and correspondence.

Authority and the Ethic of Honesty

One area of concern in the secondary literature nevertheless requires consideration, for it represents a major alternative to the interpretation of the Jung/Freud conflict presented here. In *The Triumph of the Therapeutic* Philip Rieff presents an interpretation of Freud that contrasts Freud's "analytical attitude," his "severe and chill antidoctrine," to the "modes of consolation" (Rieff 1968:30) offered by his "successor critics," Jung, Reich, and D. H. Lawrence. According to this interpretation, Freud's stature in our world derives precisely from his successful and uncompromising resistance to the temptation to be the prophet of a new religion: he will not be the spokesman for yet another (this time, psychological) version of the great Western myth of fall and salvation. "The normality of disillusion and a controlling sense of resignation," in contrast,

> which was the most for which Freud had hoped, appeared to Jung the beginning rather than the end of therapy. He proposed to continue beyond the point where Freud felt any honest analyst must leave off. Therefore, Jung went about his self-appointed task of finding new "meaning" for it all, and was paradoxical enough to be at once analytic and religious. (Rieff 1968:43)

The analytic and religious "meaning" that Jung was presumably "dishonest" enough to pursue led him to attempt "a psychotherapeutics that leads beyond itself toward a reintegration of our culture," a reintegration this time based on the recognition that "every man and every culture has, built in, a god term." Rieff continues:

> The object of therapy, in the Jungian sense, is, therefore, to reconcile the individual to whatever authority he carries within himself. Such an authority is inescapable; the wise man adapts himself to it. Indeed, in therapy one seeks just that authority which experience, now set in a confusedly antiauthoritarian frame, has hidden from the individual, sick to that degree in which he cannot find the authority directing his inner life. (Rieff 1968:45)

In other words, Rieff sees Jung developing an understanding of authority that rests on the discovery of an autonomous, inner object, and that the basic choice a person faces is one of developing a positive or negative, cooperative or uncooperative relationship to it. How Jung himself faced this choice will be discussed in chapter seven.

This choice is for Rieff not the one that confronted Freud, who, in Rieff's interpretation, appears to maintain a more complex and critical attitude to authority than does Jung. For Freud, authority represents a set of demands that come not from within but from without, i.e., from culture and the religious and ideological systems that support it. In following the course described above, Rieff states, "Jung could not have moved any further than this from Freud's position. Culture, Freud thought, may be inherently authoritarian; but just for this reason it is the interminable task of analysis to break the strangleholds of authority on the psyche" (Rieff 1968:46). Thus, in Rieff's interpretation of Freud, the authority of psychoanalysis derives from its resistance to the authoritarian demands of culture, and Freud's personal authority rests upon his fearless refusal to succumb to some myth of the "meaning" of it all.

It is Freud's refusal on this point that becomes the basis of the distinction Rieff draws in *Freud: The Mind of the Moralist* between Freud's "ethic of honesty" and the ethic of "sincerity" that Rieff feels is advocated by such figures as Carlyle, Nietzsche, Sorel, and, in the twentieth century, Jung. These advocates of sincerity, according to Rieff, are essentially romantics, and their quest is for religious forms and mysteries. Freud's alternative to romantic sincerity is "talk—

9

thorough, ruthless talk." It is Freud's "honest talk" that "fills the gap in ideals" and "creates the condition of a new personal integrity" (Rieff 1979:320). It is also precisely this "verbal honesty" that enables Freud to resist the "doctrine, myth, works of art" that "in their plenitude express [for Jung] the vital credulities necessary to the creative life" with an ethic of honesty that "demands only the negative capacity to achieve and retain unbelief" (Rieff 1979:321). In other words, Rieff's claim is that it is Freud's method, with its reliance on "thorough, ruthless talk," on "verbal honesty," that shields him from the temptations of consolation, and consequently forms the basis of his personal authority.

But what would happen if, at the crucial moment, Freud chose silence? The quotation with which this essay begins shows Freud avoiding thorough, ruthless talk precisely to preserve his authority. At a later point I will argue that Freud's authority rests not on speech at all, but on silence and the presentation of an image, a truly radical departure from the ideal of talk. Freud is not, in my view, committed to a program of personal emancipation either through honest talk or rational analysis. He seeks, rather, to exercise a historically decisive mastery over the emergence of meaning in the life of the individual. This project of Freud's implicates him in a form of romantic pessimism, described by Nietzsche as the desire to impose the experience of one's own suffering on others.

The Question of Anti-Semitism

Did anti-Semitism play a role in Jung's relationship to Freud? This question has recently been examined at length within the Jungian community (Maidenbaum 1991). But it was Freud himself who first raised the issue in his persistent search for the means to make psychoanalysis appear to be less a product of East European Jewish intellectuals. At the same time, Jung's numerous comments concerning the nature of the Jewish character (CW 10:18) and of "Jewish psychology," made near the beginning of Hitler's rise to power, require extraordinary, and singularly disingenuous, feats of interpretation to make them into anything other than anti-Semitic pronouncements. Indeed, Jung's devoted follower, Erich Neumann, accused Jung of anti-Semitism from his own self-imposed exile in Jerusalem. One can add to this evidence, from transcripts of Jung's seminars in the 1930s, that a number of his close followers at that time were sympathetic to Hitler. By 1936, however, these transcripts show Jung's increasing misgivings about events in Germany and a tendency to attack the "German psychology" as much as he might have earlier made remarks about "Jewish psychology." In the later stages of the crisis in Europe Jung made a number of analytic assessments of the dictators (see especially McGuire 1977, pp. 155 and 136) and dissociated himself from their activities.

Following the war Jung was unusually candid in his assessment of how greatly all Europe shared responsibility for what happened in Germany under Hitler. But Jung never truly takes on the issue of anti-Semitism beyond saying that his prewar remarks were made in an effort to preserve the vestiges of the psychoanalytic movement in Germany. This failure to attempt a deep investigation of the nature of anti-Semitism is singularly inexplicable in Jung. It appears now that Jung shared with many other non-Jewish intellectuals and academics what may have been a low level, and essentially inarticulate, anti-Semitism that he briefly allowed to have an impact on events that he did not anticipate. After the dimensions of the terror became evident, Jung took in many Jewish refugees from Germany. Without becoming deeply entangled in the nature of anti-Semitism, my assessment of Jung on this issue is as follows: Jung was limited in his comprehension of anti-Semitism as an essential current in European culture, and, despite his lifelong study of religious symbolism, he could not grasp the significance of political symbolism that focused on anti-Semitic themes. He was also blind to his own ambivalence toward Judaism. Once the reality of anti-Semitism became evident to Jung — and this took some time, let it be said — he turned away from it as decisively as he could and sought to escape from its confines. Thus I do not take Jung to have been an active or vociferous anti-Semite. He was, on this point, a creature of his times. And like many others, in every European nation and in the Americas, he failed to meet the greatest crisis of the Western tradition in the twentieth century.

But what of the relationship to Freud? This is a very difficult point to grasp because of Freud's own ambivalence about his Jewishness. The record on this issue is becoming increasingly clear (Rice 1990, Robert 1976, Yerushalmi 1991). There is a persistent question of whether Freud was not himself an intellectual anti-Semite. But, in the relationship with Jung, I do not believe anti-Semitism played the important role others have attributed to it. The content of the struggle lies elsewhere, although its resolution, in the formation of myths, has results that can be tied to later developments in the culture, including the anti-Semitic explosion beginning in 1933. Let us leave the matter, for now, at this: anti-Semitism poses a critical problem for understanding the Western philosophical and religious traditions. To the degree that Freud and Jung are significant figures in those traditions, they must eventually be accounted for within the problematic of anti-Semitism, especially given their particular roles. This essay does not encompass this issue. The present analysis should, however, shed light on how anti-Semitism works among other overarching cultural forces, insofar as the essay develops a theory of the origins, characteristics, and functions of myths that are in conflict with one another, and that threaten to destroy one another. With this in mind, let us turn directly to the problem of myth in the association of Jung and Freud.

Two

From Freud to Mythology

I. Jung's Dissertation

The Medium of the Unconscious

When Freud's *The Interpretation of Dreams* appeared in 1900, one of the first readers of the book was the young medical student C. G. Jung, who immediately began to incorporate Freud's insights into his own thinking. Not being under the direct influence of the master, however, Jung found his way to a point of view that, even at this early stage, distinguished his vision of the psyche from Freud's. The first public presentation of his approach was his dissertation, "On the Psychology of So-Called Occult Phenomena," that appeared in 1902. Jung used many of Freud's ideas concerning sexuality in this study, but only as one component among others. The true harbinger of his own development was the postulation of a teleological moment in the activity of the psyche.

Jung's dissertation discusses the psychology of a female somnambulist, designated for reasons of clinical discretion, Jung claimed, by the initials S. W. Her occult abilities primarily consisted of the production of "spirit" voices representing several deceased persons, some known to other members of the seances and others not known to them. One difficulty with the dissertation, however, is that Jung's claims of clinical discretion, certainly an acceptable practice, cloak a deeper level of interest that makes discretion border on dissimulation. S. W. was, in fact, Helene Preiswerk, Jung's cousin on his mother's side. And Jung did not merely observe the seances, he actively participated in them, along with other members of his family, including his mother.

Some six years younger than Jung, Helene seems to have held something of an adolescent infatuation for him. As a consequence, reconstructions of the seances by other members of the family emphasize Helene's particular attention to the young psychologist, a factor that the dissertation does not address. Jung's reluctance to acknowledge this point continued into his old age when, in his autobiography, he asserts that Helene — even at this point he remained vague and evasive about who the somnambulist really was — died in a psychologically deteriorated state at the age of twenty-six, when she actually died at the age of thirty in apparently normal psychic condition. Jung also evades his close familial relationship to the medium and makes other comments on the frequency of his encounters with her after the seances that are not borne out by other sources (Hillman 1976). This leads us to question Jung's analysis of the occult phenomena and to ask why he would indulge in the extended and rather unclinical tendency to suppress data concerning this important moment in his career.

This line of questioning grows out of the point of view taken up in chapter one, concerning Freud's shipboard dreams, where an intimate relationship between biography, concealment, and authority was suggested. To develop this theme, we will now have to grasp how it is that the teleological interpretation of Helene's seances was not limited to her own growth but pointed to Jung's development as well. We will then be able to understand the significance of the texts of both Freud and Jung in terms of their highly self-referential, mythic function. That function, in turn, will be brought under a new interpretative scheme, which I call metabiography, that questions how meaning is attributed to any biography at all. The metabiographical project is thematic for the rest of this essay, as I work out an interpretation of the biographical foundations of psychoanalysis by way of the interaction of the existential drama and mythic self-images of the two protagonists. The first step, however, requires that we examine Jung's early theories.

Teleology of the Psyche

As already noted, Jung's innovative contribution in the dissertation is a theory of the psyche as teleological, that is, as tending toward some identifiable future state of affairs in the life of the person under consideration. Jung's claims concerning teleology owe their origins as much to nineteeenth-century developments in German biology as to his interests in spiritualism, often alleged by critics to have been his only inspiration. Later, Jung's medical training leads to his understanding of the psyche as a self-regulating or homeostatic system, for which he unquestionably owes a debt to the great French physiologist Claude Bernard. But in the case of his sense for the teleological nature of the psyche, his intellectual precursors include such figures as Johann Friedrich Blumenbach and Karl Ernst von Baer, who in turn trace their theorizing to Kant's *Critique of Judgment* (Lenoir 1982). As was the case with these precursors, Jung disputes the explanatory power of Darwinian theory from a point of view of completeness and function. This in turn means that he is already at odds with Freud's Darwinian (and frequently Lamarckian) understanding of development. The key notion in this alternative tradition in biology, and the central issue in its teleomechanical worldview, is the concept of self-organization. The telos, if you will, of the organism, is its organization and the fulfillment of the functions of its parts.

In the case at hand, Jung interprets the emergent personalities of the teenage medium teleologically, in the sense just developed, as expressions of the natural maturation of an adolescent. Helene was fifteen-and-one-half at the onset of the spirit visitations, and the phenomena persisted with diminishing intensity for about two years, finally ending when Jung caught her trying to fabricate the events of a seance. In her somnambulistic phantasies, Helene frequently presented herself as the reincarnation of a woman who was so ancient that she could justifiably be called the mother of nations. Almost everyone seemed descended from her. According to the dissertation, the name of this "true" personality was "Ivenes," and Jung's interpretation of the phantasy shows a clear debt to Freud:

> But the patient's reincarnation theory, in which she appears as the mother of countless thousands, springs, in all of its naive nakedness, straight from an exuberant fantasy which is so very characteristic of the puberty period. It is the woman's premonition of sexual feeling, the dream of fertility, that has created these monstrous ideas in the patient. We shall not be wrong if we seek the main cause of this curious clinical picture in her budding sexuality. From this point of view the whole essence of Ivenes and her enormous family is nothing

15

but a dream of sexual wish-fulfillment, which differs from the dream
of a night only in that it is spread over months and years. (CW 1:120)[1]

Thus the telos that Jung explicitly claimed for this psychic experience was Helene's transition to adulthood. It manifested itself not
only in the person of Ivenes but also in other grave and forceful
figures speaking through Helene. At the same time, an extremely
childish "spirit," the psychic embodiment of the passing childhood of
the medium, challenged this maturation process. Jung is careful
throughout the dissertation to distinguish these primary phenomena
from many of the mystical and cosmological pronouncements of the
"spirits" that probably derived from cryptamnesiac recollections carried over from the waking state. While this fact complicates interpretation of the phenomena, it does not prevent Jung from concluding
that teleology is central to the situation. He summarizes his theory in
the following terms:

> It is, therefore, conceivable that the phenomena of double conscious-
> ness are simply new character formations, or attempts of the future
> personality to break through, and that in consequence of special diffi-
> culties (unfavorable circumstances, psychopathic dispositions of the
> nervous system, etc.) they get bound up with peculiar disturbances of
> consciousness. In view of the difficulties that oppose the future charac-
> ter, the somnambulisms sometimes have an eminently teleological
> significance, in that they give the individual, who would otherwise
> inevitably succumb, the means of victory. (CW 1:136)

Several points in this passage require comment. First, we can
clearly see Jung's understanding of the teleological nature of the
psyche at work. Purpose inheres in the adaptive nature of the som-
nambulism insofar as it allows Helene to survive and come to full
development of her psychic parts. We see here the notion that what
appears to be a psychic disturbance might be the solution to a problem of adaptation, albeit a potentially unstable solution, rather than
simply a symptom of an underlying pathology. In other words, as
early as the dissertation Jung, following a teleological line of reason-
ing, is playing with the idea that what Freud and others would reject
as neurotic behavior may have a positive, adaptive role to play in the
psychic economy. Furthermore, the notion of double consciousness in
somnambulistic phenomena is strikingly similar to the dissociation of
consciousness in schizophrenia, the area to which Jung devoted much

of his time in his early research. Finally, there is a sense in this passage that the emergence of deep psychic contents are premonitory. As with his teleological model, Jung's sense of the premonitory is often mis-understood. His position, here as well as later in life, is first that the unconscious is simply more aware of the direction individual develop-ment is taking and anticipates developmental events through cultur-ally coded forms such as the seance. By recalling a "deep past," in the seances the subject is able to project a developmental strategy for her future life. The importance of this futural, projective sense of psychic experiences, already developed in the dissertation, will be explored in detail below. At this point, however, I want to argue that something more is at stake in the teleological claims Jung makes for the appear-ance of these occult phenomena, something that bears more directly and more personally on his relations with Freud than a disagreement over the nature of biological transformation.

Jung's Dual Personality

We begin to appreciate the true significance of the seances when we learn, in his autobiography, that from an early age Jung was con-vinced of the existence in himself, and in certain other individuals such as his mother, of two personalities. What he referred to as the "number 1" personality was a relatively banal little Swiss boy, while the "number 2" personality was an ageless and wise old man. The emergence of the ageless mother of nations in Helene's seances thus fits into a pattern of associations already established in the young psychologist's mind. The presentation of a dual feminine character, by a close relative on his mother's side of the family, would have an even more profound meaning for Jung, as will become clear later in this chapter.

To understand the dissertation's significance in Jung's early devel-opment, it is sufficient to say that the experiences he recorded as coming from Helene — multiple personalities and great age and wisdom — mirrored experiences he had as a child but had never described in any public setting. The dissertation, on the other hand, allowed an analogue of his own experience to come forward. But his later record of the significance of the dissertation, and the events it describes, continues to present a deceptive view. Jung writes:

17

> All in all, this was the one great experience which wiped out all my earlier philosophy and made it possible for me to achieve a psychological point of view. I had discovered some objective facts about the human psyche. Yet the nature of the experience was such that once again I was unable to speak of it. I knew no one to whom I could have told the whole story. Once more I had to lay aside an unfinished problem. It was not until two years later that my dissertation appeared. (MDR 107)

The crux of the issue is that the publication of the dissertation gave Jung a means to make public an aspect of his own interior world without having to acknowledge his participation in the phantasy. This scientific presentation of a personal experience is then described as the achievement of Jung's own psychological point of view. The notion that he had "discovered some objective facts about the human psyche" indicates that his personal development, as a respectable scientist, is tied to finding the means objectively, but nevertheless covertly, to present representations of his own interior states. This view leads to the conclusion that the teleological aspect of the mediumistic pronouncements was not associated with Helene herself but with the interpretation given the seances by Jung. Thus the ultimate telos of the seances was the making of C. G. Jung into a psychologist. This involved the use of the dissertation to objectify a set of symbols and concepts, such as the primal woman and dual personality, which would serve Jung in his chosen field of medical psychology. As we proceed, this pattern of thinking will be developed and its importance will become clear. It is first necessary, however, to expand our sense of the significance of the occult, another theme that is persistent in Jung's experience and writings.

The Occult

Jung describes the occult, somnambulistic phenomena of the seances in terms that draw heavily on the experience of hypnosis. The medium is in "a semi-hypnotic state," and in fact phenomena similar to those analyzed by Jung can easily be induced in a person under hypnosis. But the hypnotic state is a curious psychic condition and is subject to extreme distortion caused by the interaction of the subject with the hypnotist. This tendency to intersubjective distortion is even more the case in a situation such as a seance. There the experience of the "occult" provides a unique venue for the emergence of a personal sense of meaning as the seance creates an emotionally charged environment dislocated from the commonsense understanding of one's place in the world.

Thus, a phenomenology of occult occurrences such as seances or classical texts dealing with the occult — for example, those of Agrippa von Nettesheim or Paracelsus — reveals the assumption of a transtemporal realm out of which the ultimate forms of self-understanding emerge. John Dee's conjuring of the dead is a dramatic symbolization of this system of meaning, and one that repeats itself, in a sense, in Jung's experience of the unconscious following his break with Freud (see chapter seven). To discover one's place in a world populated by occult phenomena is thus to leave behind one's normal relationship to time and death as, for example, Helene becomes timeless in her phantasy of primal motherhood.

Moreover, the "occult" distorts intersubjective relationships in an unusual manner. In the case before us, the very term *medium* points up this form of distortion. One person becomes an intermediary between the living and the dead. And at the same time, the "dead" come to shape the self-understanding of the living. Thus, through the medium, the temporal and the atemporal or transtemporal "interact" with one another. But the occult is distinct from the conventional religious encounter of the temporal and the atemporal precisely in the unique personal status claimed by the medium. In the present case, the dual personality of Helene and, as we have seen, of Jung himself are both possessed of unique authority when the timeless personality emerges. All of these characteristics lend themselves to the constitution of a personal mythology or system of symbolic representations that shape and inform the comprehension of time and patterns of action.

At the same time the occult is profoundly alienating just at that point where personal meaning crosses over into the realm of the timeless. To attain the status implicit in the comprehension of the occult, a portion of one's self-understanding must displace itself into a private or secret world. Only then, in the emotionally charged experience of the seance, can this highly meaningful element of the personality enter into a universe of discourse. In this way, personal meaning is implicated in the constitution of a mystery, for the cold light of rationality is antagonistic to the basic structure of the occult.

Still, the significance of the occult for Jung remains obscure at this early point in his career. On the one hand, the transtemporal nature of meaning can easily be seen in the alleged continuity of the individual beyond the grave. Personality number 2 is in some sense vindicated. But, on the other hand, Jung does not become an explicit occultist. He seeks just the opposite role, in the rational discourse of psychology. This might be accounted for first by the necessity to interpret the phenomena of the seances for presentation in the dissertation, and also by the postulation of a more appropriate or deeper meaning to life when one confronts a mystery; both are elements of occult experience that Jung can draw on to build his psychological system.

But this seems to be contradicted when we view the dissertation from the perspective of the autobiography, where it is itself interpreted in a manner that further obscures or mystifies the events rather than illuminates them. The dissertation is a concealment of the meaning of the occult events, and the autobiography is a concealment of the concealment. It is as if the entire project is one of encipherment intended to protect the mystery of the meaning which Jung originally attached to the seances. If this is the case, we may have a new vision of the continuity of meaning through time and of the role of the occult in the production of a cryptogram or anagram by a major historical figure, such as Jung, that results in the continued investigation of his life and work in an effort to break the code. This is not meant to depreciate the personality of the historical figure. On the contrary, what I want to claim is that the works and actions of someone like Jung, and, as I will show, Freud as well, are so mythic and self-reflexive, for all their claims to scientific objectivity, that they can only be seen as expressions of what I am terming metabiography. In Jung's case the occult provides the raw material for the constitution of a mystery concerning his life; and mystery serves as the place or locus of actions and interpretation. Thus my conclusion is that the dissimulations of the dissertation set up the field for the emergence of the meaning of Jung's personal experience.

Metabiography

Thus far, we have noted that both Freud and Jung adopted stances of disclosure and concealment regarding their personal experiences. On the one hand, both explicitly base and validate their statements about the human psyche by reference to their personal experiences. In doing so, each claims to possess criteria (incest, wish-fulfillment, archetype, collective unconscious) that provide a bridge between the individual and universal by distinguishing essential from circumstantial, or common from idiosyncratic, experiences. Again, in the case of both Freud and Jung, we now begin to see, the criteria for making these judgments are based on those experiences that are disclosed and taken to be revelatory and paradigmatic. Both Freud and Jung move from (1) individual personal experience to (2) the academic disclosure of general principles based on that experience, that (3) in turn provide the means of insight into the personal experiences of others. Thus Freud's self-analysis is the basis for the generalizations and subsequent dream analyses undertaken in *The Interpretation of Dreams*, and Jung's self-explorations, particularly during his "encounter with the unconscious" also provide a map for others to follow in their explorations of the depths of the psyche. On the other hand, we have also seen that at crucial points in their lives each of them suppressed information about himself. Freud not only refused to disclose a few biographical details to his chosen heir on board the ship, but throughout his life and writings he presents only partial, fragmentary accounts of those parts of his life that form the basis of his theories; and Jung consistently concealed the facts of his relationship to Helene Preiswerk, as well as important information on other cases and associations that influenced his theories. Freud's stated reason for doing so was to preserve his authority, and it is possible that a similar concern motivated Jung, since revealing his personal involvement with the medium would have called into question his credibility as a scientist. Thus, while both Freud and Jung deploy representations of their activities as scientific investigators that rely for their validity on claims to the special epistemological status of their personal experiences, it is clear that not all experiences are appropriate, and some experiences may even undermine their claims to authority. As a result, it is obvious that control over which experiences are made public is critical both for the content of psychoanalysis — that is, for determining what sorts of data are significant — and for the authority of the founder(s).

The concept of metabiography clarifies the significance of biographical information in the development and validation of psychoanalysis. In what follows, I use the concept in three senses, which correspond to the threefold structure of experience, generalization, and insight outlined above. The concept refers (1) to the role of an exemplary life in the definition of true biography; (2) to the movement from the definition of a biography to the definition of a project of attributing meaning to other lives by appeal to a system of generalization (e.g., psychoanalysis); and finally, (3) to reflection on the nature of biographical meaning in general.

The first sense of the term is at work at the end of the last section, where Jung's description of his cousin and of their shared occult experiences exhibits characteristics such as reflexivity and concealment that draw the reader into a meaning-laden encounter with Jung as an exemplar of biographical meaning. The case of Freud presents another example of this phenomenon; the exemplary and definitive status he accorded his self-analysis is of central concern as I argue that it becomes a symbol of the means and limits of access to the unconscious, the ground of valid attributions of meaning in psychoanalysis. What Jung and Freud are providing, in other words, are "mysteries" in a classical, religious sense. The mysteries of access to the unconscious give rise to rites of initiation, edification, and illumination. These rites, we will see, point to horizons of understanding where temporal orientation is of the utmost importance.

Thus the first sense of metabiography concerns how historically decisive or exemplary figures represent themselves (or are represented by others) so that their lives can become universal and determinative of the possibilities of meaning for others. This movement of an individual biography to the position of a metabiography, that is, to the status of a biography that defines the necessary characteristics of other biographies — in the case of Freud, for example, the temporal orientation of biographical self-understanding, as I will show in detail below, must be retrospective — brings us to the second sense of metabiography.

At this second level the emphasis shifts from the exemplar to the rule or system — from the exemplary characteristics of a particular metabiographical account such as Freud's or Jung's life narrative to generalizations derived from that account that define the characteristics of a public discourse such as Freud's psychoanalysis or Jung's depth psychology. This generalization from the individual to the universal takes place by way of the formation of a myth. By exploring the myths developed by both Freud and Jung in depicting their lives, we will see that both give accounts of human genesis and development that, while validated by appeal to their personal experiences, nonetheless describe systems of meaning that transcend their personal life narrative and offer an account of the origin of biographical meaning in general. Thus the second sense of metabiography concerns the question of the very possibility of biographical meaning. A rhetoric of primordiality and genesis is necessary here; both Freud and Jung provide such a rhetoric in abundance.

Recognition of the mythic, primordial grounds for the attribution of biographical meaning in psychoanalysis brings us to the third sense of metabiography. Here we confront metabiography as the project of reflecting on the phenomenon of biography itself and on the conditions of its possibility. At this reflective level metabiography seeks to answer the question: Why are there biographies at all, why not simply chronologies? At this point metabiography becomes an element in an ontology of the biographical. Taken to its conclusion, metabiographical reflection seeks to link the concrete biography of an individual to universal, perhaps transcendental, structures of self-understanding.

Having provided an outline of this organizing concept we face a project of reflection on the encounter between two individuals whose life narratives exercise an unusual fascination for our age. To put the issue more abstractly, metabiographical reflection on the grounds for the attribution of biographical meaning in psychoanalysis focuses our attention on the relationship between Jung and Freud as an encounter between two distinct systems of biographical meaning. Each system resists the other's interpretation of the basic categories of biography. As Ricoeur observes in *The Symbolism of Evil*, "The world of symbols is not a tranquil and reconciled world; every symbol is iconoclastic in comparison with some other symbol" (Ricoeur 1967:354). The result is a struggle that ultimately centers on access to the unconscious, the direction of individually experienced temporal orientation, and the nature of the symbol. It is a struggle in which each protagonist seeks to vindicate his interpretation by means of a process of universalization that takes the form of creating a culturally dominant mythology.

In the chapters that follow I shall argue that in attempting to carry out this process of universalization, both Freud and Jung act at decisive moments in accordance with the ceremonial rites associated with the system of meaning, the myth, they are attempting to defend. The most critical example on which we will focus is an enactment of the primal murder of the father as postulated by Freud in *Totem and Taboo*. Jung's struggle with Freud thus takes place in a labyrinth of biographical interpretation in which both action and thought, as the constituent elements of biography, shape two alternative systems of meaning that go far beyond the experience of the individuals involved by taking the form of myths. The metabiographical turn from the individual to the universal thus establishes contact with the hermeneutical issues described above, but with a new dimension now added to the classical notion of hermeneutics: that of the existential performance of the myth of psychoanalysis in the encounter between Jung and Freud.

II. Leonardo da Vinci

Leonardo Announced

On October 17, 1909, Freud wrote to Jung announcing the initiation of his study of Leonardo da Vinci. The announcement was portentous, for both men were striving to extend the boundaries of psychoanalysis by subjecting ever greater aspects of human experience to the technique. Mythology loomed large in both their minds, and only three days before Freud's announcement Jung had written of his obsession with the thought of a comprehensive work on the subject, hoping that Freud would "cast a beam of light in that direction" (FJL 252). Freud responded with his announcement:

> I am glad you share my belief that we must conquer the whole field of mythology. . . . We must also take hold of biography. I have had an inspiration since my return. The riddle of Leonardo da Vinci's character has suddenly become clear to me. That would be a first step in the

realm of biography. But the material concerning L. is so sparse that I
despair of demonstrating my conviction intelligibly to others. (FJL
255)

Freud clearly has in mind two areas of investigation, biography and
mythology, but the identification of one with the other is also
implicit in his discussion. Consequently, we must raise the question
of how, exactly, to distinguish one subject from the other. As I will
show, there is good reason to believe that the distinction simply drops
out in psychoanalysis. To put it another way, biography turns into
mythology almost immediately upon taking the psychoanalytic turn.

Identification of the ambiguous role of mythology in the psychoanalytic interpretation of a biography, especially when it is tied to
art and the rich world of psychical representations art provides, has a
twofold quality to it. On the one hand, we learn something about the
objects that are being interpreted. On the other hand, we begin to
learn something about the psychic state of the person doing the
interpreting. Indeed, the interpretation itself is a complex formation
of the unconscious of the interpreter. We have already seen how this
was the case in Jung's dissertation. There we saw how Jung's already
developed personal phantasy was shaping his interpretation. Can we
discern a similar pattern in Freud's encounter with Leonardo?

Freud's Egyptian Myth

One is struck, upon turning to the *Leonardo*, by Freud's reliance on
the *Hieroglyphics of Horapollo* as an interpretative tool. This text,
like so many others in the Renaissance, was thought to be of great
antiquity, providing insights into the meaning of Egyptian writing.
In fact, it was of Hellenistic origin and, like the Hermetic writings,
had little or nothing to do with ancient Egyptian culture. Nevertheless it was one of the most widely read sources in the tradition of the
prisca theologia, the ancient theology, that was all the rage among
Renaissance intellectuals. In this role it came to influence the interest
in emblems that increasingly occupied the time of the occultists
(Yates 1964:163). Freud's interest in the *Hieroglyphics* focused on
the description of the vulture which, he argues, inserts itself into an
open place in Leonardo da Vinci's childhood memories (SE XI:82).
Citing Leonardo's comment that as a child in the cradle a vulture

came and struck his lips several times with its tail, Freud remarks that this "would not be a memory of Leonardo's but a phantasy, which he formed at a later date and transposed to his childhood" (SE XI:82). The source of this symbol, for that is what the vulture becomes in Freud's account, is most likely the *Hieroglyphics of Horapollo*, which Freud was convinced Leonardo would have encountered given his wide ranging interests and the prominence of the *Hieroglyphics* at the time. Freud uses the vulture motif as an entry into a consideration of the *Hieroglyphics*, where the vulture is depicted as a representation of the essential mother, who is fecundated by the wind rather than by a male vulture since, according to the ancient text, "there is no male in this species of animal" (Boas 1950:62).

Indeed, what better symbol could there be for the child, left in his early years without a father, to be raised by a loving and lonely mother? Freud pursues this clue with vigor, putting on all the while a spectacular display of his scholarship. The only problem is that Leonardo is not talking about a vulture in his memories at all; his memory is of a kite. In his introduction to *Leonardo*, in the Standard Edition of Freud's works, Freud's translator, James Strachey, discusses this problem and attributes it to inaccurate translations of da Vinci's notebooks and to the biographer Merezhkovsky's book about the artist, upon which Freud relied heavily. In both cases the German *Geier*, vulture, is used rather than *Milan*, the proper word for kite. Strachey notes that this error forces Freud's Egyptian connection to drop out of his interpretation. He nevertheless holds that the discussions of Leonardo and of Egyptian lore have great value independent of one another (SE XI:61). My claim, however, is that the Egyptian connection is essential for understanding the study, since it is Freud's particular attachment to Egypt that is illuminated by its association with a great artist. In keeping with the concept of metabiography, *Leonardo* is first of all about Freud and only about da Vinci at one or two removes. Just as the figure of Moses overpowers any interest Freud might have had in Michelangelo, so the prospect of Leonardo's attachment to Egypt becomes, for Freud, the central issue.

Leaving aside the fact that a kite could quite reasonably have landed on the cradle of the infant Leonardo, where a vulture could not, we find Freud misconstruing Leonardo in a manner that allows him to pursue his own systematic ends. And these ends, I now want to show, concern Freud and not Leonardo or even the psychoanalysis of art. Rather, having found a point of access to Egypt by way of the *Hieroglyphics of Horapollo*, Freud is able to link his theories of the confused expectations of the child about the sexuality of the mother to the mythology of the androgynous Egyptian goddess Mut (SE XI:93). Then, by means of a transposition of field and ground, Freud asserts that the foundations of the Egyptian mythology are located in infantile sexual phantasies (SE XI:94). This series of interpretative moves, from Leonardo to the *Hieroglyphics* to mythology to infantile sexuality, severely strains the sense of biography, psychoanalytic or otherwise. Indeed, this interpretative pattern supports the claim that the juxtaposition of biography and mythology in the letter to Jung was not accidental. Biography, for Freud, moves decisively into mythology, and we are able to discern the following dialectic at work. Because biography moves into mythology, mythology becomes biography—or metabiography—in that the interpretation in *Leonardo* and the interpretation of Leonardo are elements in the formation, by Freud, of a theory of the foundations and limits of biographical self-understanding in our age.

We must add another element, however, if we are to clearly see what is at stake in this metabiographical dialectic. By turning to Jung's reaction to Leonardo the problem will be brought into focus, since Freud's study did not come to Jung simply as a text in psychoanalytic theory but also as a complex commentary on his own life and his relationship to Freud, that is, precisely as material for the mythic interpretation of their actions.

Jung's Reaction to Leonardo

Throughout the months of Freud's work on *Leonardo*, Jung said nothing concerning it, although Freud frequently complained in his letters to Jung of not having enough time to complete his research. Finally, in June of 1910, Jung responded to his first reading of the study:

> Leonardo is wonderful. . . . I have read [it] straight through and will soon come back to it again. The transition to mythology grows out of this essay from inner necessity, actually it is the first essay of yours with whose inner development I felt perfectly in tune from the start. I

would like to dwell longer on these impressions and brood quietly on the thoughts which want to unroll in long succession. (FJL 329)

Jung was at this time already at work on his major project on mythology, *Transformations and Symbols of the Libido*, and so in his clear recognition of the role of myth in Leonardo he is, in part at least, anticipating Freud's movement toward his interests. Freud's reply to Jung, however, misses the point that what matters to Jung is the place of myth in the elaboration of biography. Freud is "overjoyed at your interest in Leonardo and at your saying that you were coming closer to my way of thinking" (FJL 331). Freud is referring, at this point, to Jung's long-standing objection to the theory of infantile sexuality. But Jung's enthusiasm for Leonardo goes deeper than the problems of theory that he shared with Freud. Leonardo serves as well as a means of interpreting Jung's mythology about himself as it does to reveal Freud's latent self-image, and it therefore puts us on the threshold not only of a conflict of interpretations, to use Ricoeur's phrase, but of a confrontation between mythologies, that is, between entire systems of thought and action.

III. Jung's Mythology

Jung's Childhood Phantasies

We have already noted that the self-image Jung claimed to have developed early in life was of himself as possessing two personalities, No. 1 being the little Swiss boy from a poor parson's family while No. 2 was an infinitely old man of great wisdom. Jung saw his mother sharing this deep duality as well, and they were able, in his retelling of it, to communicate in terms of the deepest paganism of antiquity. His father, the Christian minister, was excluded from this experience. This situation raises the question of how Jung perceived himself in the context of his religious experience as well as in relation to his father. We must also ask about the accuracy of Jung's account of his sensed place in the world, since his autobiography is a deceptive account of his life experience. What I now want to show is how Jung's response to *Leonardo* illuminates these issues.

We may begin to understand Jung's self-image, and its place in his work, by exploring two momentous dreams, or visions, of his childhood. The first occurred when Jung was about three and followed upon a confusion of the Jesuits, for whom Jung's father and his clerical colleagues held a considerable contempt, with the figure of the savior Jesus. Jung records that the apparent cannibalism of the Eucharist already confused him; its association with the dark and mysterious identity of Jesuit and Jesus—for this was the pattern of association in his mind—added to his wonder. In a dream that came to him at this time, and which he never told to Freud, this confusion of the evil man-eating nature of the deity was transposed to a chthonic earth-penis that the exploring dream child finds in an underground chamber. The huge phallus is seated on a throne and, coming from above, Jung hears his mother call out, "Yes, just look at him. That is the man-eater!" (MDR 12). "I was never able to make out," Jung goes on,

> whether my mother meant, *"That* is the man-eater," or, "That is the *man-eater."* In the first case she would have meant that not Lord Jesus or the Jesuit was the devourer of little children, but the phallus; in the second case that the "man-eater" in general was symbolized by the phallus, so that the dark Lord Jesus, the Jesuit, and the phallus were identical. (MDR 12)

In the end, Jung's conception of Jesus continued to be shaped by this vision of the dark and awful side of the divinity. Jesus became, in some sense, a god of death, and the black costumes of his attending ministers contributed to this image. Among the ministers of the god of death, of course, was his own father.

Jung's other visionary experience came later in his childhood at about the age of eleven. As he left school one day, he saw before him the blue sky and the beautiful cathedral, above which sat God on his throne. At this point he stopped the phantasy vision because of the premonition that the next thought to come would constitute an unforgivable sin against the Holy Spirit. On the third night after the beginning of the vision he finally allowed himself to think through to the end what was insistently coming to him:

> I gathered all my courage, as though I were about to leap forthwith into hell-fire, and let the thought come. I saw before me the cathe-

dral, the blue sky. God sits on His golden throne, high above the world and from under the throne an enormous turd falls upon the sparkling new roof, shatters it, and breaks the walls of the cathedral asunder. (MDR 39)

To Jung, this vision was an expression of God's grace, but he never spoke of it until late in life, despite its evident importance to him.

Jung and His Father

The immediate and lasting impact of these experiences was on the relationship of the child to his father. For the child, dream and vision alike pointed to the fact that the parson was not fulfilling the will of God but, by holding fast to the theological traditions that he served, was actively resisting the opportunity to learn that will. From Jung's point of view his father's bondage to tradition caused fits of depression that led to the deterioration of his father's health and eventually to his death. In their conversations, the son wanted to tell the father of the "miracle of grace" that had come upon him but found himself unable to do so. In the end, Jung came to think of his father and their relationship in mythic terms:

> My memory of my father is of a sufferer stricken with an Amfortas wound, a "fisher king" whose wound would not heal that Christian suffering for which the alchemists sought the panacea. I as a "dumb" Parsifal was the witness of this sickness during the years of my boyhood, and, like Parsifal, speech failed me. (MDR 215)

But Jung's father did not share his son's sense that he was the victim of profound spiritual suffering. He could only conceive of his situation in physical terms, appropriate to the analysis of the family doctor (MDR 215). For the son, however, the father was trapped in a dead theology. This was the deep meaning of the earlier dream and vision: "God himself had disavowed theology and the Church founded upon it" (MDR 93).

The image that emerges from Jung's recollection of his relationship to his father is of the utmost interest. An abyss opens between the two, and the cause of the abyss is the question of established theology. Doctrine blocks the direct route to God, as it blocks the direct route from father to son. But which father and which son? Jung's dual personality haunts the entire situation. On the one hand, the visionary side of Jung is provided with a unique opportunity for insight into the divine by way of the voice of his mother while he sees "God the Father" destroy his church. But at the same time these insights disrupt the son's relationship to the temporal father. This pattern continues when, shortly after Jung's father died, his mother commented in her "second" voice that "he died in time for you" (MDR 96). Jung took this to mean that the difference between the two men might have come to hinder the course of his work. That this pronouncement emanated from the "second" personality of his mother has important consequences for a discussion of Jung's mythic phantasies.

Jung's Gnostic Myth

Whether or not we accept the autobiography as an accurate description of the events and the chronology of insights, we do have, in this account, an almost perfect reproduction of a Gnostic mythology. To understand the significance of this mythology, however, we must ask what characteristics serve to define Gnosticism. Although historical Gnosticism is highly resistant to categorization, the following aspects can, for our purpose, be isolated.

1. In all forms of Gnosticism a myth of cosmogenesis occupies the center of teaching and serves an essentially soteriological function. One must understand the state one is in to transcend that state and gain salvation.

2. The cosmogony of the Gnostic is characterized by the concept of a divine accident or fall. In many of the Gnostic myths, the supernal Godhead, the god beyond the cosmos, undertakes to create a realm of first principles, the pleroma, which contains expressions of his essential qualities such as thought, silence, the Anthropos, and finally wisdom or Sophia. In most of the myths, each of these qualities is linked to a partner that acts to keep the expression of the Godhead in balance. In the case of Sophia, however, the various myths picture her as either wishing to act without her appropriate partner, in a vain attempt to duplicate the original creation of the Godhead, or as seduced by her own relection in the disordered chaos below the pleroma. In either case, Sophia falls out of the pleroma

and brings forth a monstrous and ignorant creator god who sets out to trap, through the agency of evil "archons" or powers, the lights projected out of the pleroma by the fall of Sophia. This material order apes the order of the pleroma and is the cosmos known to man.

3. The objective of Gnosticism is to overcome this state of affairs and return to the original Godhead. This necessitates the recall of the elements of light to the Godhead by awakening them to their original state. This is usually accomplished by the intervention of the Anthropos or Son-of-Man sent out from the pleroma into the material order.

4. Distinctions within Gnosticism proliferated rapidly as the sects became increasingly autonomous, reflecting the tendency of each Gnostic believer to produce his own revelation. To claim a direct and unique revelation of one's own salvation removes one from any necessary participation in a normative or authoritative community. Thus a strong tendency towards antinomianism characterizes Gnosticism.

This brief overview of some of the major characteristics of Gnosticism helps us to identify Gnostic qualities in Jung's childhood phantasies. But to understand the systematic importance of Jung's Gnostic impulse, we must move on to some of the philosophical issues present in the Gnostic system. This task is made easier if I anticipate the development of future arguments. In one sense I am seeking, in this essay, to understand a pattern of repetition. It is not accidental that we find Gnostic themes recurring at strategic points in the development of the Western tradition. Renaissance Hermeticism is one such case. Jung's psychology is another. What makes this fairly simple historical observation philosophically interesting, however, is that the repetition of the Gnostic myth serves to solve certain problems within a developing systematic and dominant discourse. This role of the Hermetic-Gnostic tradition has become the subject of an extensive literature. We now know that during the Renaissance, Gnosticism in its Hermetic and alchemical form was instrumental in the rationalization of science. It also shaped the Reformation, which in turn gave rise to much of modern social theory (see Dobbs 1975 and Yates 1978). Jung's application of Gnostic categories, grounded in his personal Gnostic myth, to the systematic discourse of psychoanalysis performs a similar function. Specifically, Gnostic myth, and the interpretations it made possible, relate directly to Jung's struggle with the "archontic" Freud. And we can clearly see how the conceptual framework of Gnostic myth shapes Jung's interpretation of the encounter.

With this in mind we may return to the philosophical investigation of Gnosticism, which will further our understanding of Jung's childhood and his subsequent relationship to Freud. A number of writers on Gnosticism inform our philosophical interests. Hans Jonas, for example, finds the key to the Gnostic enterprise in the doctrine of the "call from without" which contains an account of human entrapment in the material world and of the means by which he may escape from it. The call motif is so strong in some of the Gnostic sects that Jonas is willing to refer to them as "religions of the call" (GR 74). Jonas summarizes the role of the call:

> The gnosis transmitted by the message and compressed in it into a few symbolic terms is the total cosmogonic-soteriological myth within whose narrative the event of this message itself constitutes one phase, in fact the turning point with which that total movement is reversed. (GR81)

At the heart of this conception of the call is a vision of the self that focuses on the sensed unity of the person with the alien God. For, as Haart puts it, "Gnosis is knowledge of the spiritual self of the Gnostic, and of the divinity which is consubstantial with this self" (Haart 1968:375). A numinous sense of the presence of the wholly other undoubtedly characterized the Gnostic experience. But this sense of the numinous focused on a unique and solitary inner experience that could not be generalized to engage others. It is this concentration of the numinous that accounts for the other philosophically important element of Gnosticism I want to highlight, antinomianism.

The doctrine of antinomianism divides into two essential elements. The first is the separation of the Gnostic, alien God from any responsibility for a normative pattern in the world. The alien God does not legislate for the world at all (GR 271f). Taken alone, Jonas points out, this argument might seem to be little more than a hybrid form of skepticism about the existence of natural law. There is more to the argument, however, which allows the Gnostic rejection of norms to assume greater philosophical significance. The Gnostic does not argue that there is no moral order in the world. Rather, it is because the moral order is associated with this world, and is therefore archontic, that it should be rejected:

> By reason of this source the law is not really indifferent but is part of the great design upon our freedom. Being law, the moral code is but the psychical complement to the physical law, and as such the internal aspect of the all-pervading cosmic rule. (GR 272)

But what is the source of the power and authority exercised by these archontic forces? The answer lies in the second aspect of antinomianism, the role of the archons as astral figures. Gnosticism is intimately tied up with late antiquity's obsession with astrology, itself linked to the problem of the symbolization of time. In his essay "Gnosis and Time" (PEY III), Henri-Charles Puech distinguishes the Gnostic view of time from those of the Greeks and early Christians. Despite the many differences between the Greek and the Judeo-Christian views of time, and of the significance of events in time, they are both committed, Puech demonstrates, to a conception of temporal continuity. And meaning, as the persistence of a specific form of discourse or interpretation of events, is also continuous and unaltered in time (PEY III:47). This, the Gnostic will claim, is the crux of the problem of cosmic domination, and, in his search for freedom, this is the point at which the Gnostic most violently attacks the tradition. In chapters six and seven of this essay we will take up the issue of the symbolization of time in Freud and Jung, and it will become evident how dramatically Jung's Gnostic vision serves to inform that aspect of their struggle.

The crucial issues in Gnosticism, however, as they relate to Jung's discovery of his own myth, are the displacement of the archontic god by man through the sensed individual unity with the god beyond; the call from beyond; the primacy of the feminine principle united with the divine child in the constitution of the world, and in its redemption; and the bondage of meaning in the images of time. In Jung's biography these Gnostic elements are mirrored in his sense that his true personality is trapped inside a gross and material body — the little Swiss boy — but that he nevertheless receives a unique revelation — the call — from the God beyond who has nothing to do with the established theology. Indeed, the intent of the established theology is to bind us to our physical being, as in the case of his father's refusal to see anything but physical illness leading to death. Misguided, archontic theologians, and later the archontic Freud, perpetuate this attitude. Finally, the personality suited to this call relates to the mother because the father does not participate in the mystical dual nature. Thus at another level, this time defined not by God but by the mother, Jung is separated from the father. This duplicates the motif of return to the God beyond by way of the interaction of child and mother.

Validation of the Autobiography

Thus far I have held in abeyance the question of what validity we can attribute to Jung's account of this series of experiences. Let us now take up this issue, or at least begin to take it up, by returning to Jung's reading of Freud's *Leonardo*. The first question concerning Jung's supposed mythic existence as a child is what weight we can give to an account written when he was eighty-three and at the end of a long life of study in the esoteric traditions. I maintain that the excitement that Jung felt upon reading Freud's study of Leonardo, and the agreement he felt with the internal dynamics of the study, constitutes a proof text for the existence of his mythic self-image at that time — about age thirty-five. A central point of Freud's analysis of Leonardo is the role of two mothers in the artist's development. Da Vinci's painting, "The Holy Family" shows the Christ Child with "two mothers," but with no father (SE XI: 113). Similarly, Freud had remarked that Leonardo may well have identified himself with the Christ Child in the role of comforter to his mother (SE XI:90). In such a role, however, the child must in some sense replace the father. A similar motif presents itself in Jung's case:

> My mother usually assumed that I was mentally far beyond my age, and she would talk to me as to a grownup. It was plain that she was telling me everything she could not say to my father, for she early made me her confidant and confided her troubles to me. (MDR 51f)

Such confidences were not exchanged, of course, when she assumed her "second" personality. Then she taught the "second" personality of her son.

Thus, although the autobiography is not always an objectively reliable source, in the reaction to *Leonardo* we do find evidence of Jung's childhood phantasy. Moreover, the correspondence with Freud bears this out. Freud's turn to ancient myth motifs, as a means of interpretive amplification, only added weight to Jung's phantasy by showing in the Renaissance master a similar synthetic project. But at a deeper level Leonardo's life, as reconstructed by Freud, even corresponded to the particulars of Jung's myth. Greatness thus corresponded to greatness. The divine child of the Renaissance matched, at the level of the dominant life myth — dual motherhood — the divine child of modernity, C. G. Jung. It is this interpretation, carried to its conclusion, that will show us a great deal about both Freud and Jung, and also about the range of biographical symbolization available to us.

The Conflict of Mythologies

In the context of the foregoing interpretation, Jung's expression of delight upon reading Leonardo suggests that he now believed that Freud was on the threshold of an understanding of the psyche based on the relationship between biography and myth that would allow him to comprehend the true depths of Jung's experience. The only problem was that Freud, far from being interested in Jung's myth, saw in the *Leonardo* a vindication of his own Egyptian mythology. The two men key their respective mythic narratives to different phases of the study; Egyptian splendor for Freud, fatherlessness and dual motherhood for Jung. This is the foundation of the conflict of mythologies mentioned earlier.

Building on the concept of metabiography, we find in the *Leonardo*, first on Freud's part and then on Jung's, an expression of the mythic element in each life that is capable of transformation into a model of meaning for other attempts at biography. But the significance of this double mythology can only be measured as we move back into the sphere of biography and determine the degree to which myths shape action and projects of self-understanding. To accomplish this, I will argue that the limits of meaning and action established by a conflict over the nature of myth itself set the boundaries of the domain psychoanalysis seeks to define. This conflict, in the form of alternative interpretations of such psychoanalytically important narratives as the myth of Oedipus will, in turn, present us with the problem of how one gains access to the unconscious within a system of psychology.

Two texts, begun about a year after the excitement of the *Leonardo* period, are expressions of the conflict. *Totem and Taboo* and *Transformations and Symbols of the Libido* can be read as attempts to vindicate the meaning of the lives of their respective authors, by then at the height of their conflict with one another. In the process, authorship itself will become problematic within the framework of the metabiographical constitution of meaning. We must therefore turn to these texts and begin to lay out their arguments.

Three

Two Metabiographical Texts

I. Beginning *Transformations*

Symbolism

In January 1910, Jung wrote Freud that he had just completed a lecture for presentation to "several scientific societies." He continued:

> The subject was "symbolism" I have worked at it and have tried to put the "symbolic" on a psychogenetic foundation, i.e., to show that in the individual fantasy the *primum movens*, the individual conflict, material or form (whichever you prefer), is mythic, or mythologically typical. The supporting material is rather thin. The thing might have been better and more illuminating, but I don't think it was too bad. Sometime I'd like to show it to you for your advice. (FJL 288f)

This now appears to have been the first indication that Jung was beginning work on what became *Transformations and Symbols of the Libido*, later to be called *Symbols of Transformation*. The theme of mythological typification was to become central to Jung's system of psychology but, as we have seen, the strong turn to mythology was not out of step, at least in principle, with Freud's investigations. This is borne out by Freud's enthusiastic response:

> Your deepened view of symbolism has all my sympathy. Perhaps you remember how dissatisfied I was when in agreement with Bleuler all you had to say of symbolism was that it was a kind of "unclear thinking." True, what you write about it now is only a hint, but in a direction where I too am searching, namely, archaic regression, which I hope to master through mythology and the development of language. It would be wonderful if you could do a piece on the subject for the Jahrbuch. (FJL 291)

Despite all the shared enthusiasm for mythology, and we must recall Freud's continuing involvement with *Leonardo,* the strained relationship between the two men was already evident. Quite often one gets the impression from the correspondence that both grasped at any instance of shared involvement in hopes of saving the faltering collaboration. This felt sense is ironic, because the culmination of Jung's announced interest in symbols was the work that ended the collaboration.

Jung Begins Transformations

The early stages of Jung's work on *Transformations* were relatively uneventful where the relationship was concerned. By December 1910, however, Jung appeared, in Freud's eyes at least, to have become evasive about his investigations. He wrote that he would not be able to bring a copy of his paper the beginning of *Transformations* with him to the congress scheduled in Munich. Freud responded that Jung's "mysterious remarks" made him curious but that he would not intrude (FJL 378f). A year after Jung began his work, in January 1911, Freud was even more curious. He could no longer understand what he termed Jung's sensitivity on the subject of myth when he ventured to criticize Jung's ideas. Jung was actually more embarrassed by his increasing deviation from Freud's orthodoxy than genuinely sensitive to Freud's criticism. Following Munich, however, Jung came forth with something of a declaration. The "manifest forms of unconscious fantasies" were eating him alive and, he continued:

> Occultism is another field we shall have to conquer with the aid of libido theory, it seems to me. At the moment I am looking into astrology, which seems indispensable for a proper understanding of mythology. There are strange things in these lands of darkness. Please don't worry about my wanderings in these infinitudes. I shall return laden with rich booty for our knowledge of the human psyche. For a while longer I must intoxicate myself on magic perfumes in order to fathom the secrets that lie hidden in the abysses of the unconscious. (FJL 421)

Freud was noncommittal on Jung's innovation, although he had been exposed to biological cycles during his association with Fliess and had recently taken an interest in thought transference under the prompting of Sandor Ferenczi (FJL 225n8). Thus when Jung came forward with the revelation that he was devoting his evenings largely to astrology, making up charts for his patients and comparing them with the results of psychoanalysis (FJL 427), Freud could only reply that Ferenczi's experiences had humbled him on the subject of the occult and that he hoped Jung and Ferenczi could work in harmony on the subject. Toward the end of August 1911, however, Freud himself had taken on a mysterious air:

> Since my mental powers revived, I have been working in a field where you will be surprised to meet me. I have unearthed strange and uncanny things and will almost feel obliged not to discuss them with you. But you are too shrewd not to guess what I am up to when I add that I am dying to read your "Transformations and Symb. of the Lib." (FJL 438)

The cloaked reference was to the actual beginning of *Totem and Taboo*, which Freud had anticipated some months earlier (FJL 391). From this point on, *Totem* paralleled Jung's work and itself appeared in 1913, at about the same time as the complete version of *Transformations*. The hint was not lost on Jung, for he replied cautiously:

> Together with my wife I have tried to unriddle your words, and we have reached surmises which, for the time being at any rate, I would rather keep to myself. . . . I, too, have the feeling that this is a time full of marvels, and, if the auguries do not deceive us, it may very well be that, thanks to your discoveries, we are on the threshold of something really sensational, which I scarcely know how to describe except with the Gnostic concept of sophia, an Alexandrian term particularly suited to the reincarnation of ancient wisdom in the shape of ΨA [psychoanalysis]. I daren't say too much, but would only counsel you (very immodestly) to let my "Transf. and Symb. of the Lib." unleash your associations and/or fantasies: I am sure you will hit upon strange things if you do. (Provided of course, that the mysterious hint in your letter has not already done so in anagrammatic form. With that letter anything seems possible.) (FJL 439)

Freud's Response to Transformations

By the time Freud replied to Jung's letter, he had already read an early form of the first part of *Transformations* and was overjoyed to find that Jung had also determined that "the Oedipus complex is at the root of religious feeling" (FJL 441). But to say this Freud had finally to admit that he too was at work on the origins of religion, the specific area which Jung had felt was going to be his in the "conquests" of psycho analysis. There now ensued a bit of fencing on the interpretation of a specific myth. Jung was at work on the meaning of the myth of the double in the Gilgamesh epic. He hinted to Freud that he had some insight into the utterances of Utnapishtim but wanted to think about the problem before he said anything. Freud responded at length on the myth of the mortal and the immortal brothers. The answer was simple, "the weaker twin, who dies first, is the placenta, or afterbirth, simply because it is regularly born along with the child by the same mother" (FJL 449).[1] Freud cites Ehrenreich and Frazer as sources on this point and then remarks that if "there is such a thing as a phylogenetic memory in the individual, which unfortunately will soon be undeniable, this is also the source of the uncanny aspect of the 'doppelganger' " (FJL 449). Far from considering phylogenetic memory "unfortunate," Jung responded that he was becoming increasingly convinced that all the memories of early childhood could be phylogenetic in origin. There were other symbols, Jung went on, which might have their source in intrauterine experience, including water symbolism or the sense of being encoiled or of being in a strange skin (FJL 450).[2]

The Attacks

Freud was by this time in possession of a large portion of *Transformations*, toward which he was by turns noncommittal or quietly complementary. He continued to write to Jung about his own difficulties in the study of religion. Throughout the letters of this period, however, one cannot mistake the fact that Freud sensed the parting of the ways that was coming. At first both Freud and Jung attempted to cover up the problem by attributing it to different styles of work (FJL 459f). In the midst of this gentle evasion, however, Jung suddenly thrust at Freud:

> In my second part I have got down to a fundamental discussion of the libido theory. That passage in your Schreber analysis where you ran into the libido problem (loss of libido = loss of reality) is one of the points where our mental paths cross. In my view the concept of libido

as set forth in the Three Essays needs to be supplemented by the genetic factor to make it applicable to Dem. praec [Dementia Praecox]. (FJL 461)

Freud's response took an uncharacteristic two weeks to arrive—he usually responded by return mail—and complained vigorously when Jung did not do the same during which time Jung apologized for being too aggressive in his comments on the libido theory.

On November 29, 1911, however, Freud told a meeting of the Vienna Psychoanalytic Society, following a paper read by Sabina Spielrein, that Spielrein's presentation:

> provides the opportunity for a critique of Jung because in his recent mythological studies he also uses any mythological material whatsoever, of which there is an abundance in its present version without selection. Now, mythological material can be used in this way only when it appears in its original form and not in its derivatives. The material has been transmitted to us in a state that does not permit us to make use of it for the solution of our problems. On the contrary, it must first be subjected to psychoanalytic elucidation. (Nunberg 1974:335)

In his letter of response to Jung, written the next day, Freud mentions, without elaboration, that he has taken this critical step "in the discussion with the little girl" (referring to Spielrein, FJL 469), as he had also taken a stance against any thought of psychoanalysis being dependent on biology, philosophy, physiology, or brain anatomy. He then goes on to comment on Jung's suggestion that the libido theory needs "expansion" by writing:

> I should be very much interested in knowing what you mean by an extension of the concept of the libido to make it applicable to Dem. pr. I am afraid there is a misunderstanding between us, the same sort of thing as when you once said in an article that to my way of thinking libido is identical with any kind of desire, whereas in reality I hold very simply that there are two basic drives and that only the power behind the sexual drive can be termed libido. (FJL 469)

The Problem of Psychosis

Freud's question recalled Jung to a set of issues that had beset relations between the two investigators from the beginning. When they were dealing with neurosis Freud clearly took the lead and Jung willingly followed. Jung, however, was far more familiar with psychosis than was Freud. To some degree this was simply a matter of Jung's being connected with the great Burgholzli Hospital in Zurich, where he had been able to observe many cases of dementia praecox schizophrenia under the direction of the great psychiatrist, Eugen Bleuler. This distinction notwithstanding, there is, from the beginning of the correspondence, a sense in Freud that where dementia praecox is concerned his theory of sexual etiology must prevail regardless of what contrary evidence other investigators might present. The fact of the matter was that Freud had little or no direct experience with severe psychosis. The study of Schreber (1911) was an exercise in analysis at a distance, by way of reading an autobiography, but Freud nevertheless maintained that he had found the sexual etiology of Schreber's psychosis and that his general theory was thus vindicated.

Jung's first study of dementia praecox, in contrast, was written in 1907, while he was still at the Burgholzli and in daily contact with clinical cases of psychosis. His important book, *The Psychology of Dementia Praecox*, along with his internationally recognized work on the word association test, established Jung, still in his early 30's as a leading figure in experimental psychiatry. Jung nevertheless attempted to bring Freud's ideas to bear where appropriate, but the problem remained that psychosexuality did not account for all the observable phenomena. The discrepancy caused Jung to postulate a genetic, organic factor in the psychoses. He speculated that these factors resulted in the presence of chemical imbalances or the presence of "toxins" that lead to psychotic states. Commenting on the tendency of the psychotic to become fixated, Jung had written that:

> the symptoms produced by the hysterogenic affect are different from those of dementia praecox. We must therefore suppose that the disposition for the origin of dementia praecox is quite different from that for hysteria. If a purely hypothetical conjecture may be permitted, we might venture the following train of thought: the hysterogenic complex produces reparable symptoms, while the affect in dementia praecox favors the appearance of anomalies in the metabolism toxins,

perhaps, which injure the brain in a more or less irreparable manner, so that the highest psychic functions become paralyzed. (CW 3:75)

The importance of genetics, biochemical imbalances, and metabolic disturbances in the etiology of the psychoses is no longer in dispute. Jung may well have been the first to advance the notion, and he stood by his insight to the end of his life. In 1907, however, Freud would have none of it. He wrote to Jung that in the appeal to toxins Jung thrust aside the sexual etiology which Freud had been developing (FJL 19). At this early point, Jung was contrite and averred that more work certainly needed to be done. He lamely wrote "that perhaps the sex glands are the makers of the toxins" (FJL 20).

The Problem of Libido

In 1911 the same tendency to argue over fundamentals was at work, but with renewed strength and very real implications for both men. Jung's reply to Freud's call for a critique of his use of mythology acknowledged the need for care in the treatment of the subject and then turned to the nature of libido. Freud's doubt raised anew all the problems Jung had worked at in trying to solve the riddle of dementia praecox by recourse to Freud's theories. The most important problem was the loss of reality:

> The loss of the reality function in D. pr. cannot be reduced to repression of libido (defined as sexual hunger). Not by me, at any rate. Your doubt shows me that in your eyes as well the problem cannot be solved this way.[3] . . . The essential point is that I try to replace the descriptive concept of libido by a genetic one. Such a concept covers not only the recent sexual libido but all those forms of it which have long since split off into organized activities. A wee bit of biology is unavoidable here. (FJL 471)

By raising the problem of the loss of reality in psychosis and by suggesting that a genetic view of libido is necessary to solve the problem, Jung questions the status of the foundations of the psychoanalytic view of human existence. The differences that began with a misunderstanding concerning the nature of the symbol have now moved to a point where the grounds for the attribution of meaning in psychoanalysis are at issue. Jung here begins to suggest that change is possible at the most elementary level of meaning. And as the argument reaches this point, the changes taking place in the lives and works of Freud and Jung begin to function as representations of a conflict over the boundaries of meaning. This is the point, in other words, at which commonsense biography takes the philosophical turn into metabio-graphy. As we will see in a moment, a metabiographical interpretation of *Totem and Taboo* focusing on the myth of the primal horde and the primal killing, reveals that text to be an attempt to foreclose any alteration of the Freudian theory of the unconscious and, by extension, of the libido. Foreclosure itself emerges from the mythology of the primal killing. Why Freud should want to hold this position directly relates to his concern for power and authority which, in the quest for control over the constitution of biographical meaning, now moves to center stage.

Freud's Claim to Possess the Truth

Following Jung's advocacy of the genetic view of the libido, Freud takes a turn that would seem, finally, to remove any doubt Jung, or others, might hold concerning his vision of the foundations of psychoanalysis. On December 17, 1911, he writes:

> My study of totemism and other work are not going well. I have very little time, and to draw on books and reports is not at all the same as drawing on the richness of one's own experience. Besides, my interest is diminished by the conviction that I am already in possession of the truths I am trying to prove. Such truths, of course, are of no use to anyone else. I can see from the difficulties I encounter in this work that I was not cut out for inductive investigation, that my whole make-up is intuitive, and that in setting out to establish the purely empirical science of ΨA I have subjected myself to an extraordinary discipline. (FJL 472)

Freud is being ironic, but there is nevertheless the striking claim that the truth is already in his possession.

More violent, and obscure, however, is an attack Freud mounted on the author of the Book of Genesis. In her paper of November 29, 1911, which was sympathetic to Jung's concept of the transformation of the libido, Spielrein had undertaken an interpretation of Genesis. At the meeting, Freud responded by arguing that Genesis was a classic example of the distortion of a myth that could only be corrected by proper application of orthodox psychoanalytic technique. Considering that Jung was now advocating a genetic view of the libido, we can infer that Freud's attention to Genesis stands as a singularly pointed pun, especially in light of the remark he made to Jung in the letter of December 17, 1911:

> You have asked for an example of my objections to the most obvious method of exploiting mythology. I shall give you the example I used in the debate [at the November 29 meeting]. Fraulein Spielrein had cited the Genesis story of the apple as an instance of woman seducing man. But in all likelihood the myth of Genesis is a wretched, tendentious distortion devised by an apprentice priest, who as we now know stupidly wove two independent sources into a single narrative (as in a dream). (FJL 473)

In Genesis, Freud goes on, the woman gives the man the fruit in contrast to the typical motif, which one finds in the myth of Proserpina and Pluto where the man gives the fruit to the woman. If the inversion was corrected "Eve would be Adam's mother, and we should be dealing with the well-known motif of mother-incest. . . ." (FJL 473). "Consequently," Freud concludes:

> I hold that the surface versions of myths cannot be used uncritically for comparison with our Atical findings. We must find our way back to their latent, original forms by a comparative method that eliminates the distortions they have undergone in the course of their history. (FJL 473)

Freud insists that the manifest form of a phantasy or dream is not its actual meaning, unless it clearly points to the sexual character of libido in an unmistakably Freudian fashion. There is always a latent version of a myth underlying the surface form. Only the myth of Oedipus, it would seem, does not require revision since, in Freud's opinion, it is the absolute paradigm of mother-son incest. But such a procrustean approach to myth creates serious problems. The simplest way to put the issue is: Why do myths change form? Freud argues that they do not change at all in their deep structure, but only in their manifest characteristics in order to deceive. The story of Adam and Eve is simply a censored version of the incest motif. For Freud the entire system of the psyche rests on a simple description of libido and a complicated system of coding devices which seek to hide the libido's nature.[4]

On another level the question of change engages Freud's interpretation of the authorship of Genesis, and the integrity of its mythic representation of origins, in a consideration of Freud's own mythic self-image. While Freud might have been in good scholarly company insofar as he was attempting a text-critical assessment of the fragmentary nature of the writing of Genesis, the tradition concerning Genesis, the myth of Genesis, we can say, holds for its authorship by Moses. The intense concentration both Freud and Jung were applying to mythology at this time, as well as the strange violence of Freud's attack on the authorship, compels us to reject the notion that Freud was simply trying to give a historical account of the authorship. On the contrary, the attack on the authorship of Genesis, interpreted against the background assumption of Mosaic authorship, is an attack on the legitimacy of a non-Oedipal, that is non-Freudian, foundation of meaning. Moses stands, for Freud, in the position of the traditional lawgiver and eventually, particularly in *Moses and Monotheism,* becomes a part of Freud's complex Egyptian mythology. At the point where Freud attacks the author of Genesis, therefore, Freud's interpretation crosses over itself as Freud's personal vision of authority comes to rest in his claim to possess the truth. To make this claim, Freud must displace all other agents engaged in the articulation of a myth of origins. Thus the passage concerning the writing of Genesis is self-referential at the same time that it is undoubtedly intended to be a critical reference to Jung. This ambiguity in Freud's comment on authorship will assume a central position in the development of our understanding of the struggle with Jung when we turn to a reading of Freud's own "Book of Genesis," *Totem and Taboo*, the project which at this time absorbed all of his attention. We will then be able to understand precisely how it is that the existential drama of Jung's struggle with Freud works itself out in their writings, which assume metabiographical importance as definitions of the limits of possible biographical meaning.

To begin this portion of the analysis of Freud's system, however, I will first survey the geography surrounding *Totem* by way of guide points found in Hegel's *Phenomenology of Spirit*. This move to Hegel is motivated by two aspects of the Freudian project itself: first,

Hegel leads the way in modern philosophy to a consideration of the relationship between death and the family in the construction of a theory of the foundations of culture and authority. Freud is, therefore, an heir to Hegel in his similar effort in *Totem and Taboo*. Second, Hegel is central to the contemporary philosophical interpretation of Freud, especially in Ricoeur, Lacan, Marcuse, and Habermas. Thus Hegel will help to orient us both in terms of the systematics of Freud's analysis and in terms of the philosophical significance of Freud's system. The philosophically important result of this turn to Hegel in this essay is that the conclusion of my discussion of *Totem* we will be on the threshold of an understanding of the nature of authority as a problem of temporality. This understanding will emerge by way of a consideration of the relationship between death, the subject to which we must now turn, and the psychic mechanism of repression, the subject of chapter four.

II. Death and the Dialectic of Authority

Hegel's Vision of the Family: Law and the Unconscious

A brief overview of Hegel's argument concerning the family highlights the following elements. For Hegel, action, as the foundation of individual differentiation, begins in the family (PS 269). This differentiation takes place in relation to an otherwise undifferentiated community of individuals which, upon the emergence of the individual from the family, forms itself into the state. Such a community is governed by human law, a law that expresses the requirements of the state (PS 267). This law opposes what Hegel terms the divine law, embodied in the family and giving expression to those requirements that diverge from the interests of the state (PS 268). Preservation of a balance between human law and divine law is an essential function of ethical action.

Desire, the omnipresent motive force for both Hegel and Freud, drives the individual out of the family and into the community. Freud's vision of desire corresponds to Hegel's argument that movement away from the family is necessary for the development of the culture. As the family establishes the individual, so the community allows the individual to act ethically (PS 269). This action, in turn, provides the larger community with its unique and distinguishing character. But the essence of action on behalf of the state, that it is necessary for the existence of the community, is hidden from the individual, and the state only recognizes the individual as an actor subject to the human law. Consequently, the relationship of the individual to the authority of the state ceases with the individual's death (PS 270). Furthermore, the state cannot ground the significance of this death in anything but the elemental destructiveness of nature. So far as the state is concerned, the individual simply dies. Therefore the family, which originally formed the individual, must assume responsibility for the dead individual and give death a purposeful content that overcomes mere nature, thereby establishing the integrity of consciousness in opposition to nature. If this were not done, nature would eventually overpower the community itself.

To preserve the community and its human law, the family asserts its claims on the individual through the divine law, which introduces the dead individual into the nether world (PS 273). Hegel views rites of death as a means whereby:

> The family makes him a member of a community which prevails over and holds under control the forces of particular material elements and the lower forms of life, which sought to unloose themselves against him and destroy him. (PS 271)

The family, which originally gave the individual to the community of the living, thereby negating itself, now acts to sustain the living community by again giving up the individual, this time to the community of the dead.

What is at stake for the state in this dialectical movement of the individual is the inability of the state to provide a sense of order through its instrument, the human law, that accounts for the end of life as part of the individual's responsibility to the community. Death, in the context of the state's view of the individual, is accidental to the labors the individual has undertaken on behalf of the state (PS 270). Only through the mediation of the divine law of the family can these labors be redeemed for the community:

> Neither of the two is by itself absolutely valid; human law proceeds in its living process from the divine, the law valid on earth from that of the nether world, the conscious from the unconscious, mediation from

immediacy and equally returns from whence it came. The power of the nether world, on the other hand, has its actual existence on earth; through consciousness, it becomes existence and activity. (PS 276)

Here we clearly see, in the dialectic of the law, of the nether world, and of the world of the living, a correspondence to the relationship between the unconscious and the conscious.

As we will see, Freud connected the need for incest taboos, working against an unconscious desire to remain in the family, to the need of the larger social community to protect itself from the internal system of desires in the family. In other words, if the incest desire, as an unconscious drive, were not overcome by some institutional control, the community would never exist, as all desire would be directed to the immediate members of the family. Similarly, Hegel sees a need for the individual to emerge from the family in order to establish the state.

Freud, however, failed to account for the role of the family in guarding the community against the irrationality of death, the second moment in Hegel's view of the family. This failure on Freud's part, I want to argue, was not accidental. Rather, Freud could not posit any movement other than expulsion from the family *because the ontological status of the family gives its members access to the unconscious*, as Hegel makes clear, *and it is Freud's project*, I now want to argue, *to deny access to the unconscious*. Thus, to follow Hegel, in according the family the right to reclaim the individual from the state and pass the individual on to the nether world, to the unconscious, Freud would have to relinquish his exclusive claim to have defined the nature of the unconscious. Precisely why this should be the case will become clear as we proceed. We may anticipate, however, by observing that Hegel, drawing on Sophocles' *Antigone* rather than his *Oedipus*, placed the woman in the leading role at the rites of entry into the world of the dead, the funeral, and in a similar vein, both Freud and Jung see the nether world of the unconscious as presided over by the woman, a claim the significance of which will become clear in chapter five.

Furthermore, while Hegel did not give adequate consideration to the fact that his favorite theatrical heroes, Oedipus and Antigone, were both involved in incest, he nevertheless provides us with valuable clues for a deep understanding of the place of law, of authority, in the analysis of the unconscious. The key continues to be the role of the family. For Hegel, Sophocles' masterpiece, *Antigone*, was "one of the most sublime presentations" of the virtue of family piety (PR 114 [A]). This virtue, which ultimately sustains the individual against the forces of nature, is characterized in the *Philosophy of Right* as:

> the law of the ancient gods, "the gods of the underworld"; as "an everlasting law, and no man knows at what time it was first put forth." (PR115[A], citing *Antigone*, II, 450–7)

Hegel thus directs us to a primal stratum of "law" in the realm which psychoanalysis designates as the unconscious and which Freud claims is without the benefit of law. As will be argued later, this claim on Freud's part reflects a refusal to deal with the ambiguity of incest because of the systematic ends which recognition of that ambiguity would seriously undermine. In the case of Antigone, and here I depart from Hegel, we see that it is precisely the product of Oedipus's incest, Antigone herself as the ideal representation of the unconscious, who bestows a blessing on the community, as Oedipus also did at the moment of his death.

This is not to say, however, that we can find an analysis of the meaning of incest in Hegel. On the contrary, he seems to have sought, in the person of Antigone, a representative of sexual purity.[5] What Hegel does offer is a vision of the family that, despite its superficial resemblance to Freud's analysis, allows for an understanding of incest and the unconscious that is dramatically at variance with Freud's. Again, the crucial issue is the place of law in relation to the unconscious. For Hegel a dialectical conception of the law is possible, wherein the unconscious plays a positive role. Freud rejected this view. To understand why, we must return to Freud's analysis of incest.

Oedipus as the Signifier of Culture

In 1920 Freud added a footnote to his small but important book of 1905, *Three Essays on Sexuality*, which defined the intensity with which he viewed the Oedipus complex:

It has justly been said that the Oedipus complex is the nuclear complex of the neuroses, and constitutes the essential part of their content. It represents the peak of infantile sexuality, which, through its after-effects, exercises a decisive influence on the sexuality of adults. Every new arrival on this planet is faced by the task of mastering the Oedipus complex; anyone who fails to do so falls a victim to neurosis. With the progress of psychoanalytic studies the importance of the Oedipus complex has become more and more clearly evident; its recognition has become the shibboleth that distinguishes the adherents of psychoanalysis from its opponents. (SE VIII:226)

What is the history of this immutable psychoanalytic truth? Freud's earliest known reference to Oedipus as a paradigm of psycho-sexuality is his letter to Fliess of October 15, 1897. There he attributes the gripping nature of the Greek drama to the universally shared experience of incestuous desire (SE I:265). The horror felt by the audience is an expression of the disjunction between childhood phantasy and adult life, which is the result of repression (SE I:265). What finally convinced Freud that this was the case, however, was the discovery of the incest desire in his own psyche during his self-analysis.

Freud's discussion of Oedipus in *The Interpretation of Dreams* rejected, as had his letter to Fliess, the typical interpretation of the tragedy as one of fated disaster brought on by man's attempt to evade the judgment of the gods. The key to the drama, Freud maintained, was the community's shared recognition of the unconscious desire to engage in incest. Added to this was Freud's observation that the dramatic progression of the play was strikingly similer to the stages of psychic insight and development encountered in the course of psychoanalytic treatment (SE IV:262). In the end, Freud contends, "the text of Sophocles' play sprang from some primeval dream-material which had as its content the distressing disturbance of a child's relationship to his parents owing to the first stirrings of sexuality" (SE IV:263). By concentrating on the theme of primordiality in this passage, we may expand our understanding of the place of myth in Freud's system. As Laplanche and Pontalis observe:

even in this first formulation Freud spontaneously refers to a myth transcending the history and the variations of the individual life-experience. He asserts the universal validity of the Oedipus complex from the very first, and will adhere to this thesis ever more firmly as time goes on. . . . (LP 283)

Indeed, as early as 1905, Freud saw the Oedipus drama as the linchpin of cultural development. The incest taboo, he writes in the *Three Essays*, is "essentially a cultural demand made by society" that prevents the family from assuming priority in the individual's life (SE VII:225). Incest taboos result in object selections that contribute to the formation of larger social groups by compelling separation from the family. While this brings with it an overcoming of the dominance of parental authority, the pattern of object-choice defined in the Oedipus motif continues to govern the life of the individual (SE VII:227).

The Turn to Totem and Taboo: *Patriarchy vs. Matriarchy*

In 1905 Freud had not completely developed his theory of incest. He had not, in fact, determined where or when the incest taboo originally emerged. This issue was finally taken up in *Totem and Taboo*. It cost him great mental anguish, and he later remarked to Jones that the anguish reflected the difficulty of the move from the theoretical killing of the father to his actually being killed (Jones 1957, II:354).[6] The analysis that takes place in *Totem* falls into two phases that continue the disjunction between theory and act. The first, based substantially on the work of Frazer, is a proof for the general prohibition of incest in primitive societies. For Frazer, and for Freud, the "horror of incest" was a universal aspect of cultural development. The second movement in the analysis is the postulation of a reason for the universality of the taboo. Freud accomplished this movement by way of the famous story of the primal horde, which he drew out of a combination of Darwin's observations of apes and his own analysis of the phantasies of modern man. It is in the primal horde that the sons' wish for the mother, and the resistance of the dominant male, or patriarch, results in the deed of displacing the father by killing him. Killing is followed, in Freud's reconstruction, by a cannibalistic feast wherein the now dead father is represented by the mythology of a totem animal whose sacrificial rites become, in turn, the foundation of religion.

While Freud admits that the exact form of patriarchal social organization assumed in his hypothesis had never been observed, he claims that the lack of such evidence should not be taken as a contradiction of the theory (SE XIII: 141). Patriarchy, according to Freud, simply defined the primal form of social organization even if there was some sort of matrilineal pattern on the surface. Jung, on the other hand, had begun to develop a theory of primal matriarchy under the influence of J. J. Bachofen's *Das Mutterrecht*, a book that Freud had dismissed as inadequate (FJL 503f). This was not an incidental point of scholarship. On the contrary, it orients us toward a basic aspect of the structure and function of the incest motif in the elaboration of psychoanalysis. Freud's basic answer to criticism coming from supporters of the "matriarchal" alternative focuses on the view that the Oedipus complex is definitive for the person's relationship to the object of desire, no matter what the social system is in which this desire is expressed. The mother is the "first love object" (SE XVI:329) and as such defines the relationship of the subject to what we might call the object-of-desire-in-general. Desire is thwarted by the patriarchal father, who thereby becomes the representative of prohibition-in-general. The conflicts bred of the failure of the initial incest wish set in motion the mechanisms of repression, which account both for the sense of taboo and for the displacement of desire to the sister, or some other proximate sexual being, who replaces the faithless mother (SE XVI:334).

The key to Freud's theory, however, is the need to kill the father rather than simply to develop a displacement or otherwise avoid the problem. This is the actual deed that he mentioned to Jones, and it tends to undermine attempts to rescue Freud from inadequate anthropology by recourse to systematic generalization. In other words, Freud does have an investment in the reality of the primacy of patriarchy in the history of culture. If the father were simply that individual who "possesses a mother sexually" (FJL 504), there would seem to be little reason for the "mob of brothers," or the modern psychoanalytic patient, to experience the profound ambivalence towards the father that results in the father being killed and then venerated in the totem feast, with its concomitant prohibition on any further killings motivated by incestuous desires. The patriarch is essential to Freud's theory.

Killing and Death

We are now in a position to work out the mechanics of the incest taboo in a manner that will resume the dialogue with Jung. At the heart of *Totem* we find neither a theory of the psyche nor even a theory of religion. What we do find is a general theory of patriarchal authority that rests on death, just as Hegel's theory of the vindication of law or authority rested on death, but without the possibility of the ceremonial mediation found in Hegel. Such mediation is precluded by the fact that in *Totem* Freud argues that the primordial experience of death in human culture is not an indifferent act of nature at all, but rather a willed act, a killing. From this point on, we must constantly hold this fact in mind since, for Freud, the experience of death as killing establishes the law and is thus the basis for a system of authority.

This state of affairs is not lost on Freud's commentators. We have already seen how Hegel juxtaposed the two moments of death and law in the formation of a culture; Laplanche and Pontalis seek an analogous juxtaposition on behalf of Freud by working out of Jacques Lacan's Hegelianized reading of Freud. To understand this juxtaposition we must remember that it is the wish for the mother that leads to the killing of the father:

> Its [the Oedipus complex's] efficacy derives from the fact that it brings into play a proscriptive agency (the prohibition against incest) which bars the way to naturally sought satisfaction and forms an indissoluble link between wish and law (a point which Jacques Lacan has emphasized). (LP 286)

This association of incestuous wish leading to killing of the father and the emergence of a system of authority persists to the end in Freud's work, and we may therefore profit, by way of perspective, from a brief look at Freud's late view of the Oedipus complex. The reason for gaining a more distant vantage point is the need to have clearly in mind not only the intensity with which Freud viewed the complex, as is shown in the footnote to *Three Essays* cited above, but also the range of phenomena that he subsumed under it. In this manner, we can clearly discern the social role of the complex and distinguish it from Hegel's view. In the later works, for example, the superego assumes the function of cultural development. But this is really nothing more than an elaboration and refinement of the motif of the totem feast in that it perpetuates the influence of the parents in the psychic life of the individual (SE XIX:25). As such, the superego is the "heir to the Oedipus complex and has thus introduced the most momentous objects into the ego" (SE XIX:38). To further spell out this relationship Freud recalls the 1913 hypothesis of the primal horde and explicitly ties it to the superego in his 1930 study, *Civilization and Its Discontents*. The remorse of the sons that follows upon the killing of the father continues to be the essential ingredient in the building of culture:

> It [the feeling of remorse] set up the super-ego by identification with the father; it gave that agency the father's power, as though as a punishment for the deed of aggression they had carried out against him, and it created the restrictions which were intended to prevent a repetition of the deed. . . . So long as the community assumes no other form than that of the family, the conflict is bound to express itself in the Oedipus complex, to establish the consciousness and create the first sense of guilt. (SE XXI:132)

This passage clearly illustrates the conflict between Hegel and Freud. For Freud, the family is essentially at variance with the interests of society but is nevertheless biologically essential as a means of bringing forth the components of that society. Freud does not see, even in 1930, when death has come to occupy a central place in his investigations, any requirement for the family to mediate the experience of death. Instead, Freud introduces another element, the sense of guilt. This leads him to one of his most pessimistic formulas:

> Since civilization obeys an internal erotic impulse which causes human beings to unite in a closely knit group, it can only achieve this aim through an ever-increasing reinforcement of the sense of guilt. What began in relation to the father is completed in relation to the group. If civilization is a necessary course of development from the family to humanity as a whole, then as a result of the inborn conflict arising from ambivalence, of the eternal struggle between the trends of love and death there is inextricably bound up with it an increase of the sense of guilt, which will perhaps reach heights that the individual finds hard to tolerate. (SE XXI: 133)

The power of this argument, which derives from *Totem*, lies in the fact that it introduces a high level of tension in the interpretation of death by moving the decisive experience of death into the primordial past while at the same time encompassing ever larger social groups under the rubric of guilt. Consequently, guilt intensifies as the experience of the primal killing is distributed throughout one's experience of the highest forms of culture and the broadest distribution of intersubjective interests. Eventually, wherever one looks one confronts the recollected primal killing. But here we find yet another aspect of the Freudian vision of death. Insofar as the killing of the primal father and its attendant guilt defines our relationship to death, it is a death remembered and not a death anticipated. Furthermore, this view of the place of death transforms the repressive authority of the father into the foundation of civilization. Guilt, born of rebellion against this primordial repression, continues to build upon this foundation to give us the structure of a culture.

Freud departs decisively from Hegel's vision. Lacking the "everlasting law" of Antigone, death for Freud signifies nothing more nor less than a transgression against the law of the father. Indeed, in Freud's version of the primal killing it is the sons, not the women, who are responsible for the rites of death for the father, and it is out of those rites that totems and taboos arise. But Freud's view of the law reduces the legitimate objectives of culture to a unity in that all cultural activity is intended to achieve reconciliation with the repressive demands of the father. This means that there can be no dialectic of the law for Freud as there is in Hegel. Everything depends on the father. There is only the iron necessity of repression.

This monistic foundation of human experience brings to light another crucial element in Freud's argument. If one follows the logic of Freud's project to its end, one must conclude that all death is essentially killing. To put it another way, under the cold light of primordial guilt one can only construct a meaningful interpretation of death by seeing it to be a murder. While Hegel had found death meaningless under the rule of human law and dependent on divine law, as mediated by the family, to give it meaning, Freud finds death meaningful as the foundation of civilization and the source of law, but only if it has the form of a killing. Furthermore, the necessity of interpreting death as killing is itself a response to the experience of the primordiality of repression, to which we must now turn.

Four

Repression

I. Freud's Argument

Repression and the Unconscious

Coming to terms with Freud's understanding of repression is among the most difficult tasks in developing an interpretation of psychoanalysis. What is often missed in discussion of repression is that its central role in Freud's theory derives not only from its clinical significance as a defense mechanism but also from the role repression plays in determining the structure of the psyche itself. In a word, Freud's argument concerning repression is an argument concerning the processes that establish the topography of the psyche and carry out the interactions within the psyche.[1] For Freud, in the first stages of his theoretical development, such terms as *conscious*, *preconscious* and *unconscious* defined the topography of the psyche. Later, the terms *id*, *ego*, and *super-ego* replaced the earlier topography. Freud used a variety of metaphors to capture his vision of the mechanisms of interaction within the psyche, but among his most persistent metaphors were the economic terms of *investment* and *disinvestment*, which, in the English translations of his works have come down to us as *cathexis* and *de-cathexis*. Another term, which has considerable significance for this discussion is *anti-cathexis*, in effect, refusal to invest.[2] These processes are of particular importance to us because an understanding of the role of repression in Freud's model of the constitution of the psychic topography will help define the nature of the interaction between force, which is expressed in repression, and meaning, which is inhibited by repression.

Throughout his career Freud refined, qualified, and dramatically altered his description of the processes at work in his system. Consequently, formulating generalizations about his insights is difficult. By way of beginning, however, we find that Freud postulates two forms of repression: 1) primal repression and 2) repression proper (sometimes referred to as after pressure). Only the second form is of daily concern to the clinician, because it is the causal agent behind those repressed wishes and memories that reassert themselves in the neuroses. However, what is often missed in clinical as well as many theoretical discussions of repression is that repression proper does not take place only because the higher levels of mental activity, the preconscious or the conscious levels, reject objectionable wishes and memories, sending them into the limbo of the unconscious. Rather, Freud's observations convinced him that already repressed contents in the unconscious exert an attractive force on those elements of experience that later become repressed. Furthermore, he postulated that the unconscious itself could only exist if repression were already taking place. This means that some account must be given of the origins of the unconscious, and that account must accommodate the mechanisms of repression. It is at this level that primal repression becomes important for our understanding of Freud.

The Constitution of the Unconscious

In 1915, shortly after the final break with Jung, Freud wrote the "Papers on Metapsychology." Among them is one titled simply, "The Unconscious." Concerning this paper Paul Ricoeur remarks that its purpose is to "make the concept of the unconscious plausible" (FP 117). This points to an often overlooked distinction which Ricoeur goes on to clarify:

> The movement of thought [in the paper] leads from a descriptive concept, where the term "unconscious" is an adjective, to a systematic concept, where it becomes substantive; the loss of its descriptive meaning is indicated by the abbreviation Ubw, which we translate as Ucs. To arrive at the topographic point of view is to move from the adjectival unconscious to the substantive unconscious, from the quality of being unconscious to the unconscious as a system. (FP 117f)

Keeping this distinction in mind allows us to proceed to one aspect of Freud's definition of the unconscious as a system (designated, as Ricoeur notes, by the abbreviation, Ucs, as Freud designates the Preconscious and the Conscious systems by the abbreviations, Pcs and Cs respectively) that will allow us to take hold of the problem of the constitution of meaning by way of the emergence of a structure of representation in the system Ucs:

> The nucleus of the system Ucs. consists of instinctual representatives which seek to discharge their cathexis; that is to say, it consists of wishful impulses. (SE XIV:186)

The concept of the "representation of an instinct" is a necessary element in any attempt to understand Freud's project, and it is at the heart of his dispute with Jung. As an examination of Freud's paper, "Instincts and Their Vicissitudes," shows, there are strong philosophical currents surrounding the concept of instinctual representation that make of the instincts something very much like Kant's thing-in-itself. Like the thing-in-itself, the instincts themselves are boundary conditions. The instincts do not present themselves to us in unmediated form. Rather, they manifest themselves through their object of satisfaction, or by some other psychic or ideational representation such as a dream image. Because the instincts are built into the organism we can never escape them, but their representations, which mediate our awareness of their actions, can be subjected to the many forces at work in the psychic apparatus. Some of these forces change the representation of an instinct into new paths that are more culturally acceptable by way of sublimation. Alternatively, repression can set in when the representation of the instinct is too inappropriate and the instinctual drive, along with its representation is then driven back into the unconscious.

A complication remains, however, for Freud is not clear on how the representation of an instinct comes to be given in the unconscious in the first place. This problem at first points in the direction of the phenomena of infantile sexuality, because Freud contends that at the earliest stages of development, aspects of childhood experience are discarded into the unconscious (SE XIV:195). These "infantile repressions," which draw on the primal phantasies of parental intercourse, castration, etc., are expressions of archaic instinctual activity. But the logic of Freud's system requires an even more archaic or primordial act of repression by which the systems Ucs and Cs are constituted in the first place, since it is only in the presence of both systems that representations of the instincts are subjected to the vicissitudes of repression in the first place. Thus we return to the problem of the origins of the process of repression and the genesis of the unconscious.

The Two Forms of Repression

The first step in understanding the mechanism of repression is the realization that it is not based simply on the application of force on the part of the conscious mind. There is, to repeat, an attraction, one might say a seduction, exerted by the unconscious as well. Indeed, "the trend toward repression would fail in its purpose. . . if there were not something previously repressed ready to receive what is repelled by the conscious" (SE XIV:148). As already noted, this aspect of Freud's theory makes it necessary for him to posit two forms of repression: repression proper (*Verdrängung*), which designates the expulsion of conscious contents into the unconscious, and primal repression (*Urverdrängung*) "which consists in the psychical (ideational) representative of the instinct being denied entrance into the conscious" (SE XIV:148). Such a primordial denial of access establishes a fixation, an unalterable attachment of the instinct to a particular unconscious representation (SE XIV:148). This means that an instinct, which would normally find different representations at different stages of development, becomes attached instead to an immature or infantile representation which at a very early stage is declared inappropriate and therefore suitable for rejection. Furthermore, as an infantile representation, it never enters consciousness. It is at this point that the distinction between the systems Ucs and Cs is established and becomes the basis of subsequent acts of repression.

A certain sense of a *deus ex machina* is evident at this point, but at the same time one must acknowledge Freud's problem as that of any attempt to discuss "first things." Laplanche and Pontalis draw attention to this dilemma when they write that "the Freudian unconscious is *constituted* even if the first stage of repression (primal repression) may be considered mythical" (LP 475) though it is based in experience. If we are indeed dealing with a "myth" of primal repression, then what we confront at this point is Freud's cosmogony, which, we recall, is a fundamental aspect of the struggle with Jung. Thus, despite its obscurity and Jung's similar obscurity about the role of projection in constituting the "world" of the psyche, we are here on the threshold of a crucial aspect of any understanding of psychoanalysis.

Repression and Guilt

In 1930, in *Civilization and Its Discontents*, Freud arrived at a deeper vision of the fundamental nature of repression:

> It now seems plausible to formulate the following proposition. When an instinctual trend undergoes repression, its libidinal elements are turned into symptoms, and its aggressive components into a sense of guilt. (SE XXI: 139)

We have already noted that an essential link exists between *Civilization and Its Discontents* and *Totem and Taboo*. I now want to claim that *Civilization* is in fact a working out of issues raised in *Totem* that allows us to locate the latent components of the earlier work in such a way that we will see the primacy of repression and the critique of repression as the foundation of the system of psychoanalysis.

The notion that guilt is an essential concomitant of repression suggests that primal repression has an aggressive component that brings with it a form of primal guilt. This notion, needless to say, brings to mind the primal horde and primal killing, i.e., the drama of *Totem and Taboo*. Precisely this point is taken up by Jacques Lacan, who sees the killing of the primal father as the metaphor constitutive of the entire structure of the conscious and the unconscious and as an analogue of primal repression that stands, for Freud, "at the level of the constitution of the unconscious" (Lacan 1968: 271f). For Lacan, the Oedipus complex, founded on the killing of the father, allows the child to metaphorically acquire the phallus of the father as a sign that the child has taken over the father's function. The phallus then becomes the fixated image that means, as Freud would want to claim, that the quest for the origins of the unconscious leads to the Oedipal wish to kill the father and possess the mother. This conclusion cannot be emphasized too strongly. What we find, in Freud, is truly a myth of origins, a Genesis of the most fundamental of realities for psychoanalysis, the unconscious.

But if the Oedipus complex and its primal representation, the phallus of the father, lie at the foundation of the system Ucs, what do we learn from Freud concerning the other systems of the psyche, the systems Cs and Pcs?

Consciousness and Guilt

At the beginning of his metapsychological essay, "Repression," Freud argues that repression is "primarily a stage of condemnation, something between flight and condemnation" (SE XIV:146). As such, it really "interferes only with the relation of the instinctual representative to one psychical system, namely, to that of consciousness" (SE XIV:149). In other words, it is only the system Cs that finds instincts truly objectionable or contradictory and must therefore act to counter them. But we can see an important aspect of the problem of the constitution of the conscious here. Condemnation is another form of the consciousness of guilt, and, therefore, in the constitution of the conscious we must identify the notion of primal guilt. If we continue to follow the notion that primal repression is part of a "myth" of the origins of the system Ucs, then the mechanisms of repression may also lead us to a "myth" of the origin of the system Cs.

This combination of myths would mean that there is an argument in Freud's metapsychology for something akin to the doctrine of original sin. Existence precedes the unconscious; consciousness arises out of a sense of guilt, which is itself a falling away from the primordial truth. Consciousness is therefore a state of deprivation since the guilt that actually constitutes the conscious system is the guilt that accompanies primal repression, the representation of which is forever hidden, trapped in the unconscious. As we will see, Freud's interpretation of the relationship between conscious and unconscious is not as extraordinary as it may at first seem. But at this point all we see in Freud is a peculiar vision of consciousness as a system hemmed in on all sides by other structures that radically circumscribe its limits and define its shortcomings.

This impression of the contingent nature of consciousness intensifies in the *Introductory Lectures* (1916), where Freud develops his
extended metaphor of the censorship as the watchman at the door of
the room containing the system Cs. This watchman intervenes to
prevent unsavory characters from the unconscious from entering the
room. Even if one of the unconscious characters succeeds in passing
the censor, it will not necessarily catch the eye of consciousness. Thus,
Freud introduces the preconscious as yet another level in the psychic
topography. The preconscious, at first sight, seems to be simply the
container of those psychic characters to which consciousness has
momentarily turned its back, to continue the metaphor, and therefore there would not seem to be any reason why consciousness could
not at some point take them up for consideration (SE XVI:245f). But
the preconscious is also laden with machinery because it is the censorship that is the mechanism of repression proper. The censorship is the
ultimate judge of the acceptability of the unconscious characters, of
whether they are fit company for consciousness. This is not the whole
story, however. Consciousness considers the contents of the preconscious to exhaust the sum of psychic material that it could absorb and
at the same time rejects some of those contents as objectionable. To
account for this rejection of some preconscious contents, Freud introduces a second censorship between the preconscious and the conscious systems. In the end, Freud concludes that:

> to every transition from one system to that immediately above it (that
> is, every advance to a higher stage of psychical organization) there
> corresponds a new censorship. (SE XIV:192)

The repeated imposition of censorships results in an extreme separation of consciousness from the vast majority of the contents of
mental life. Things are so filtered by the time they get to the system
Cs that consciousness has virtually no idea what they originally looked
like. This construct of the theory leads Freud to a remarkable and
important conclusion:

> The reason for all these difficulties is to be found in the circum-
> stance that the attribute of being conscious, which is the only charac-
> teristic of psychical processes that is directly presented to us, is in no
> way suited to serve as a criterion for the differentiation of systems.
> Apart from the fact that the conscious is not always conscious but also

at times latent, observation has shown that much that shares the characteristics of the system Pcs. does not become conscious; and we learn in addition that the act of becoming conscious is dependent on the attention of the Pcs. being turned in certain directions. Hence consciousness stands in no simple relationship either to the different systems or to repression. The truth is that it is not only the psychically repressed that remains alien to consciousness, but also some of the impulses which dominate our ego something, therefore, that forms the strongest functional antithesis to the repressed. The more we seek to win our way to a metapsychological view of mental life, the more we must learn to emancipate ourselves from the importance of the symptom of "being conscious." (SE XIV:192f.)

The problem with consciousness, insofar as it is a symptom, is precisely its lack of comprehension of the vast world that lies behind it. Therefore, if we simply rely on consciousness to define our world for us, we may justly be termed neurotic. Consciousness is, in effect, a neurosis.

Meaning and the Unconscious

Freud, in his interpretation of repression, is arguing against the primacy of consciousness. Throughout Freud's writings, one is constantly struck by the remarkable and inexplicable sensitivity of consciousness to every element of unconscious activity that approaches it. At every turn, censorships protect consciousness. Meanwhile, the unconscious exists free from contradiction, timeless, a reality unto itself (SE XIV: 187).

The relations among the psychic systems were a constant problem for Freud. They involved him in continual revisions of theory by which he sought to overcome one paradox after another. The present disparity in strength between conscious and unconscious is a case in point. This situation, however, finally opens up the Freudian system to an analysis of the constitution of meaning. To come to terms with the problems of meaning, we must again take up the notion of ideational representations of the instincts. We no longer need to attend to the instinctual level itself, however, since, having already seen how the representation of the instincts served, through primal repression, to set up the topography of the psyche, we can now attend more directly to the behavior of the representations themselves in the economy of the psyche.

Keeping in mind that for Freud the key to understanding the structure of the psyche is the fact that in primal repression instinct becomes attached to a representation that never enters consciousness, then this representation or idea constitutes, that is, actually establishes the unconscious as a system and becomes, thereby, the attractive pole for energy associated with representations that do find their way to consciousness but are nevertheless subject to repression proper. That is to say, the unconscious, as it is set up by primal repression, can absorb energetic stimulation from ideas in the conscious system and thereby leave them without meaning. This denial of meaning is the basic function of repression in that it prevents the representation of the instinct from becoming active in consciousness. The mechanics of repression thus determine the limits of meaning, or the lack of meaning, for consciousness.

However, denial of meaning by repression implies that primordial meaning is associated with the functioning of primal repression, to which we must again turn, now with an eye to the system of internal exchange. Freud writes:

> What we require, therefore, is another process which maintains the repression in the first case [i.e. the case of after-pressure] and, in the second, [i. e. that of primal repression], ensures its being established as well as continued. This other process can only be found in the assumption of an anticathexis, by means of which the system Pcs. protects itself from the pressure upon it of the unconscious idea. It is this which represents the permanent expenditure [of energy] of a primal repression, and which also guarantees the permanence of that repression. Anticathexis is the sole mechanism of primal repression; in the case of repression proper ("after-pressure") there is in addition withdrawal of the Pcs. cathexis. It is very possible that it is precisely the cathexis which is withdrawn from the idea that is used for anticathexis. (SE XIV:181, brackets in Freud's text)

Repression is thus a mechanism of power within the economics of the psyche. The economics combines with dynamics and topography to establish a complete metapsychology. But before everything else it is primal repression which, by way of anticathexis, sets up the economics (SE XIV:181) as it denies to consciousness any opportunity to effect an investment, cathexis, in the most primordial instinctual representation. By moving to this consideration of primordial representation we come to confront the problem of meaning in its most radical form. To elaborate this point, however, we must learn more about the nature of representation in psychoanalytic theory.

Representation and the Unconscious

Ricoeur, following a widespread trend in French psychoanalytic thinking, takes the linguistic form of metaphor as the link between the systems Ucs and Cs "Metaphor is nothing other than repression, and vice versa . . ." (FP 402) he writes, on the way to arguing for Lacan's formulation that the [Freudian] unconscious is structured like a language. However, the unconscious is not itself language. Psychoanalysis seeks to bring the contents of the unconscious to language, i.e., into the domain of meaning, and the sense that this can be achieved is based on the fact that in Freud's system "there is no economic process to which there cannot be found a corresponding linguistic aspect" (FP 403). And yet, it is the economic system that "guarantees the separation of the systems" (ibid.). It is this point of separation that concerns us in this essay, for if, as Ricoeur continues:

> it is necessary, in Freud's words, that "the psychical (ideational) representative of the instinct [be] denied entrance into the conscious"; this denial, which precisely constitutes primal repression (*Urverdrängung*), is not a phenomenon of language (FP 403),

then there is a constitutive moment in the juncture between unconscious and conscious, the primal denial, that is forever outside the limits of meaning, to the extent that those limits are bounded by language. The importance of this limit on meaning is set in perspective if we recall Rieff's insistence on Freud's devotion to relentless talk and my contention, at the beginning of this essay, that Freud invokes silence at the point where his authority is at issue. Thus, to anticipate the development of this argument, we now begin to see that there exists a boundary condition that limits what can be made meaningful by way of language; and that boundary condition is tied both to the systematics of Freud's model and to the drama of his encounter with Jung. System, meaning, and personal authority depend on one another, and primal repression becomes a metaphor defining the nature of the relationship between Jung and Freud as well as a critical aspect of Freud's system.

With this formulation of the limits of meaning in psychoanalysis, we have in hand the theoretical foundation for an interpretation of the problem of authority in Jung's struggle with Freud. I propose to address this issue and show that the deep structure of authority in psychoanalysis, building on the primacy of repression, results in the denial of meaning. This denial allows us to propose that the dynamics of repression and the dynamics of Freud's vision of his personal authority are contingent upon one another and are mutually reinforcing. For repression to be, conscious access to meaning must cease to be, and for authority to be, Jung cannot be allowed to find meaning in Freud's dream.

II. Repression and Jung

Guilt and Renunciation

We have already seen that as late as *Civilization*, Freud continued to explore themes that he originally developed in *Totem*. Prominent among these themes was the association of guilt with repression. Guilt is a factor in the development of the conscience (SE XIII:67) and as such is tied in Freud's late topography of id, ego and super-ego to the formation of the super-ego (SE XXI:125). But prior to the emergence of guilt there appears anxiety, which, for Freud, is a phenomenon associated with specific circumstances. In 1900, citing even earlier work, Freud had argued that "anxiety is derived from sexual life and corresponds to libido which has been diverted from its purpose and has found no employment" (SE IV:161). In 1910, Freud was more specific: anxiety was to be seen as an action of the ego "in repudiation of repressed wishes that have become powerful" (SE XI:37) and hence as clearly tied to specific wish formations. By the time of *Civilization*, anxiety and conscience had become associated with one another, with anxiety having temporal priority in the dynamics of instinctual renunciation (SE XXI:128). Anxiety, therefore, is anxiety about something, guilt is associated with some wish, and conscience seeks out ever new objects of instinct that it can renounce. Renunciation begins under the impact of an external authority, but soon the process is internalized and a dialectic of renunciation is set up where every act of renunciation results in an impulse to renounce even more (SE XXI: 128). The entire program of guilt, conscience, and renunciation is therefore intimately associated with the pattern of repression and hence with the distinction between unconscious and conscious. Freud even acknowledges the instructive quality of the linguistic similarity in English between conscience and consciousness (SE XIII:67). The correspondence between these concepts is further strengthen when Freud locates the primal source of guilt in the repression of the two wishes associated with the primal desire and played out in the Oedipus drama: murder and incest (SE XIII:143 and SE XXI:131).

Freud as Primal Patriarch

With this we come, again, to the world of *Totem and Taboo*, but with a greater sense of the role of primal events in the constitution of the psychic world. Killing the primal father causes the murderous sons to experience remorse, a form of anxiety, which in turn gives rise to guilt. The remorse felt at the killing of the father is the result of the primordial ambivalence the sons feel for the father. They both love and hate him, and while the hate manifests itself in their killing of the father, the love rapidly returns in the form of remorse and guilt.

In both *Totem* and *Civilization,* Freud's argument assumes mythic dimensions, and as a culturally dominant myth, it has had a profound impact on the self-understanding of our age. I have claimed, however that the constitution of such a dominant myth can be subsumed under the concept of metabiography. I now propose to turn again to metabiography to show how, in their confrontation, Freud and Jung seek to settle the question of the limits of biographical self-understanding in the modern world. The first step in this turn is the rather commonplace recognition that Freud's relationship to all of his followers can be interpreted in Oedipal terms. Given this state of affairs, *Totem*, written at the same time as his relations with Jung were beginning to unravel, may be interpreted as a commentary, from Freud's point of view, on the disintegration of the collaboration. In this case, Freud can be seen as having the self-image of the primal patriarch or tyrant intent on forcing his sons—the young analysts gathered around him—into the impossible situation of the Oedipus drama. By itself, this is not sufficient to form an interesting thesis because Freud was sensitive to the Oedipal forces at work in his group. What we must look for, as a consequence, is a deeper level of interaction that will link *Totem* directly to Freud's relationship to Jung.

The key lies not in Freud's role as father to the other analysts, which is only a superficial problem, but rather in the mechanics of primal repression itself, where we will find the foundations of authority laid down in the denial of primordial meaning.

Let us begin by evaluating Freud's self-image in light of the assertion he made that Jung harbored a death wish against him. This assertion was associated with a series of fainting spells experienced by Freud in Jung's presence. One case occurred just before the departure of Freud, Jung, and Ferenczi for the United States in 1909. Freud had cajoled Jung into drinking some wine—under the influence of Bleuler, Jung had become a strict abstainer—which loosened Jung up a bit and started a conversation about the recently discovered bog men in Denmark. The conversation got on Freud's nerves and he suddenly fainted. Later, Freud remarked that he was sure the discussion of corpses reflected a death wish toward him on Jung's part (MDR 156). Another attack of fainting occurred during the Munich conference of November 1912. An attempt had been made, with some apparent success, to reconcile the two men. After having a private conversation, they returned to hear a paper presented by Karl Abraham on Egyptian religion. Jung recounts the rest of the events:

> Someone had turned the conversation to Amenophis IV (Ikhnaton). The point was made that as a result of his negative attitude toward his father he had destroyed his father's cartouches on the steles, and that at the back of his great creation of a monotheistic religion there lurked a father complex. This sort of thing irritated me, and I attempted to argue that Amenophis had been a creative and profoundly religious person whose acts could not be explained by personal resistances toward his father. On the contrary, I said, he had held the memory of his father in honor, and his zeal for destruction had been directed against the name of the god Amon, which he had everywhere annihilated; it was also chiseled out of the cartouches of his father Amonhotep. Moreover, other pharaohs had replaced the names of their

actual or divine forefathers on monuments and statues by their own, feeling that they had a right to do so since they were incarnations of the same god. Yet they, I pointed out, had inaugurated neither a new style nor a new religion. (MDR 157)

At which point Freud fainted.[3]

Freud's Desire to Die

Jung wrote to Freud following the conference in the most conciliatory tones and inquired after his health. Freud replied that he had had several fainting spells in the past and that the Park Hotel in Munich seemed to hold special difficulties for him, as he had had two of his spells in its dining room. The reference to prior fainting fits pointed back to the relationship with Fliess and, indeed, Freud remarked to Jones that there was "some piece of unruly homosexual feeling at the root of the matter" (Jones 1957, 1:317). To Jung, however, he only wrote of "a bit of neurosis that I ought to look into" (FJL 524).

Jung, returning to his earlier combative tone, reacted strongly to this remark in his next letter and provided his own analysis of what the neurosis was by reversing the accusation of a death wish:

> My best thanks for one passage in your letter, where you speak of a "bit of neurosis" you haven't got rid of. This "bit" should, in my opinion, be taken very seriously indeed, because, as experience shows, it leads *"usque ad instar voluntariae mortis"* ["to the semblance of a voluntary death"]. I have suffered from this bit in my dealings with you, though you haven't seen it and didn't understand me properly when I tried to make my position clear. (FJL 525)

Freud's testy reply to Jung on this point was simply that Jung had not "been injured by my neurosis" (FJL 530). At this point their short-lived reconciliation again came apart and culminated in the final break slightly over a year later.

The implication of Freud's reply to Jung is clearly that Freud is the one who had suffered from the neurosis. This might be the case, in part, if the neurosis were either homosexual in origin or if it related to problems in his family caused by his relationship with his sister-in-law. But the manifestation of the neurosis clearly has to do with death and the death wish aspect of the Oedipus complex which, we have seen, is intimately tied up with guilt and repression in Freud's system. Furthermore, even if Jung did wish Freud dead, only the neurosis associated with the omnipotence of thoughts (SE XIII:85) could explain Freud's fainting and that would mean, as Jung pointed out, that it was Freud who in some way wanted to die while Jung vigorously protested that he harbored no death wish against Freud.

On the larger scale, however, we must note that it is Freud's system that attaches to the killing of the father the extraordinary significance of being at the foundation of civilization. It does not figure prominently in Jung's system since, as we will see shortly, it is replaced by the need to transcend the mother. It is at this point, therefore, that we can profitably return to Lacan and the problem of signfication (language) to gain insight into what is at stake in this situation from a Freudian point of view.

Death and Law

Anthony Wilden describes Lacan's view of the relationship to the father as follows:

> The Symbolic father is not a real or an Imaginary father (imago), but corresponds to the mythical Symbolic father of *Totem and Taboo*. The requirements of Freud's theory, says Lacan, led him "to link the apparition of the signifier of the Father, as author of the Law, to death, or rather the murder of the Father, thus demonstrating that if this murder is the fruitful moment of the debt through which the subject binds himself for life to the Law, the Symbolic Father, insofar as he signifies the Law, is actually the dead Father." (Lacan 1968:270 cites "Traitement possible de la psychose" [1958], pp. 24–25; see Lacan, *Écrits* 217)

Wilden goes on to remark that:

> this primal of all primal scenes is related in Freud to the "primal repression" for which Lacan substitutes the terms "constituting metaphor" or "paternal metaphor." (Lacan 1968:270)

Lacan is clearly correct in his assertion that the law, at least in the form of taboo, is dependent, for Freud, on the killing of the primal father. This allows us to ask a fundamental question concerning Freud: Does Freud need to be killed by his "son," Jung, to achieve the final institution of his own law, his own dispensation of the law? Are we in fact, in the room where Freud faints, witnessing the creation of a myth, with its totem animal and its taboos?

The thesis I want to sustain is that Freud, viewed from the point of view of his own theory, can indeed be said to have desired to die at the hands of Jung. The association of this wish with the creation of a mythology will ultimately allow us to determine that Freud saw himself in the role of the founder of a totemic religion. The point of the argument in *Totem and Taboo* is that this religion is based on death. Furthermore, it is not simply any death that is necessary; it is the killing of the father by the son, notwithstanding that in almost all mythic situations where deaths figure prominently in the origins of religion it is the father who kills the son or allows him to be killed.[4] This fact, which has ample phenomenological and historical foundations, compels us to rethink Freud's theory in order to integrate Jung into Freud's myth. This is necessary since Freud can be seen, in his insistence that Jung give up his own conclusions, to be attempting to sacrifice his "son." But the way for Freud to achieve this and to institute the law of psychoanalysis is to induce his "son" to entertain the notion that he has a death wish against the father. This argument raises a further problem of ambiguity in the death motif: Does the culture-constituting death have the form of killing or of suicide? This ambiguity will be clarified in chapters five and seven. At this point, however, we must attend to the issue of how Jung came to deal with this challenge.

Meaning and Force: Jung's Response to Freud

Jung was writing *Transformations* at the same time Freud wrote *Totem*, and the two books may be interpreted as mutual commentaries. The analysis of repression accomplished in *Totem* can then be shown to be an attempt to overcome the system developed by Jung in *Transformations*. By way of an outline, we can say that Jung binds the libido to the symbol, rather than the symbol to the libido as Freud had done. In Jung, the symbol determines the appropriate expression of an otherwise undifferentiated libido, which thus cannot be described as being exclusively sexual. The Oedipus complex is simply one among other symbolic systems by which libido expresses itself, and even this symbol system is not unequivocally sexual in nature. It is this reading of the symbol that provides Jung with the means of escape from Freud. In *Totem,* Freud sets up the counter-argument. If Freud can constellate the death wish against himself in Jung, he will, as Lacan suggests, succeed in binding Jung to the Freudian system, that is, to Freud's law. To put it another way, he will deprive Jung of the symbols of transformation, which are necessary for escape, by subordinating all symbols to the desire to kill the father.

In *Transformations,* Jung provides himself with the means to refuse the need to entertain a death wish against Freud by asserting that the ability of the symbol to form meaning is not restricted to a single formulation and that the symbol therefore has the capacity to transform libido. The cogency of this approach to the symbol, as a solution to the problem of authority, is borne out in the analysis of the economics of the psyche outlined above. Force, in the form of the foreclosure of meaning by primal repression, becomes Freud's answer to the primacy of meaning advanced by Jung. It is essential for Freud, if he intends to maintain the integrity of his law, to find a means to overcome the system of transformative symbols advanced by Jung. Thus Jung's rejection of the charge that he harbored a death wish against Freud becomes the starting point for an understanding of Freud's system in which guilt and repression are masters over meaning. The *Essays on Metapsychology* thus become an argument for the necessary *incorrectness* of Jung's personal response to Freud. Freud is embarked on a polemic against Jung that will absorb the rest of his life insofar as twenty years later, in *Civilization and Its Discontents,* he continues to insist on the primal horde's killing of the primal father as the foundation of his theory of culture. Consequently, we may conclude our interpretation of repression by recognizing that at the foundation of Freud's system there is a pattern of behavior that is itself a ceremonial working out of a mythology of primal authority. Freud lives his theory and he seeks to make others live it as well.

Five

The Interpretation of Incest

I. The Incest Crisis

The Incest Taboo

On February 25, 1912 Jung wrote to Freud that he had "ventured to tackle the mother" as part of his investigations of incest motifs in *Transformations*. In fact, he went on, he had remained out of touch with Freud because of the "καταβασις [= "descent"] to the realm of the Mothers, where, as we know, Theseus and Peirithoos [sic] remain stuck, grown fast to the rocks" (FJL 487f). Jung, however, assured Freud that he would soon return from the underworld. In his reply, Freud did nothing more than upbraid Jung for failing to attend to the business of the International Psychoanalytic Association, in particular to the preparations for a forthcoming conference of the group. Jung became defensive at this and claimed that the approach of his annual military duty had interfered with his planning activities for the Munich meeting. He then remarked that Freud's criticism of his ideas was not well taken. He would happily bow to "one who knows better" on a particular issue but nevertheless "I would never have sided with you in the first place had not heresy run in my blood" (FJL 490). The new heresy to which Jung implicitly refers is his reinterpretation of incest from the perspective of his continued belief that sexuality did not exhaustively define the nature of libido. Shortly after the letter acknowledging the possibility of heresy, Jung wrote a long and significant statement of where he found himself in relation to incest:

I very much regret my inability to make myself intelligible at a distance without sending you the voluminous background material. What I mean is that the exclusion of the father-daughter relationship from the incest prohibition, usually explained by the role of the father as (egoistic) law-giver, must originate from the relatively late period of patriarchy when culture was sufficiently advanced for the formation of family ties. In the family the father was strong enough to keep the son in order with a thrashing, and without laying down the law, if in those tender years the son showed any incestuous inclination. In riper years, on the other hand, when the son might really be a danger to the father, and laws were therefore needed to restrain him, the son no longer had any real incestuous desires for the mother, with her sagging belly and varicose veins. A far more genuine incest tendency is to be conjectured for the early, cultureless period of matriarchy, i.e., in the matrilinial family. There the father was purely fortuitous and counted for nothing, so he would not have had the slightest interest (considering the general promiscuity) in enacting laws against the son. (In fact there was no such thing as a father's son!) Therefore I think that the incest prohibition (understood as primitive morality) was merely a formula or ceremony of atonement *in re vili*; what was valuable for the child—the mother—and is so worthless for the adult that it is kicked into the bush, acquires an extraordinary value thanks to the incest prohibition and is declared to be desirable and forbidden. (This is genuine primitive morality: any bit of fun may be prohibited, but it is just as likely to become a fetish.) Evidently the object of the prohibition is not to prevent incest but to consolidate the family (or piety, or the social structure). (FJL 502f)

Juxtaposed with the writing of *Totem* this letter makes remarkable claims indeed. To assert that the father has nothing to do with the establishment of incest prohibitions runs directly counter to Freud's vision. The truly central concept, however, is related to the object of veneration. For Freud, the ultimate recipient of veneration on the part of the son is the father who has been killed in the process of working out the incestuous drama. This killing establishes the totems and taboos of the tribe. Now Jung asserts the primacy of the mother in the structures of veneration. The father is nowhere to be seen. This distinction in their respective views of the nature and origins of religion—veneration of the father versus veneration of the mother—will prove to be of central importance.

Freud had already identified J. J. Bachofen as Jung's source on matriarchy. In his study of Oedipus in *Mother Right*, Bachofen had advanced the notion, which Freud would also develop, that the name

Oedipus ("swollen foot") had a phallic connotation (MR 180). Beyond that, however, Bachofen turns the myth inside out, in Freud's view, and asserts that it "marks the advance to a higher stage of existence" (MR 181) where the woman comes to be protected in the institution of the family. It is Bachofen's contention, in fact, that "woman in particular venerated Oedipus as the institutor of her higher condition" (MR 183). More important still, for understanding Jung's appropriation of his ideas, is Bachofen's detailed discussion of the origins of Oedipus himself. Oedipus, as Bachofen correctly points out, was of the race of Spartoi, people born out of the earth, which meant that they had "no recognized father but only a mother" (MR 180). The identification of this motif in the structure of the Oedipus myth, coupled with the letter just cited, puts us in mind, once again, of Jung's own experience of his mother as a primal being and of the relative insignificance of his father. Just as in the case of the Leonardo, Jung finds grounds in the original form of the myth or biography of the hero to vindicate his own experience. But this can only take place at the expense of Freud's hermeneutics of suspicion, which seeks to overcome the manifest form of the myth by appeal to the mechanisms of censorship and repression.

With this, the reason for the Freudian project of claiming systematic distortion becomes increasingly clear. Freud wishes to see in the incest prohibition the exaltation of the father. This brings the conclusion of Jung's letter into clear relief since, following Bachofen, Jung sees the origins of the incest prohibition as contributing to sociality insofar as it strengthens the position of the mother in the family, an argument compatible with Hegel's vision of the role of women in the family. Freud's argument, on the other hand, is that society needs incest taboos to keep the family from becoming too strong and therefore uses the taboos to drive the child out of the family while at the same time instituting a system of authority that binds the child to the will of the father.

Freud's objections to Jung's matrilinial view of incest were to no avail. Jung came forward, in yet another letter, with further revisions of the entire view of the structure, function, and disposition of the unconscious as found in Freud. We must recall the specificity attached by Freud to the phenomenon of anxiety in order to grasp the depth of Jung's continued heresy:

As regards the question of incest, I am afraid of making a very paradoxical impression on you. I only venture to throw a bold conjecture into the discussion: the large amount of free-floating anxiety in primitive man, which led to the creation of taboo ceremonies in the widest sense (totem, etc.), produced among other things the *incest taboo* as well (or rather: the mother and father taboo). The incest taboo does not correspond with the specific value of incest *sensu strictiori* any more than the sacredness of the totem corresponds with its biological value. From this standpoint we must say that incest is forbidden *not because it is desired* but because the free-floating anxiety regressively reactivates infantile material and turns it into a ceremony of atonement (as though incest had been, or might have been desired). Psychologically, the incest prohibition doesn't have the significance which one must ascribe to it if one assumes the existence of a particularly strong incest wish. The aetiological significance of the incest prohibition must be compared directly with the so-called sexual trauma, which usually owes its aetiological role only to regressive reactivation. The trauma is *seemingly important* or real, and so is the incest prohibition or incest barrier, which from the psychoanalytic point of view has taken the place of the sexual trauma. Just as *cum grano salis* it doesn't matter whether a sexual trauma really occurred or not, or was a mere fantasy, it is psychologically quite immaterial whether an incest barrier really existed or not, since it is essentially a question of later development whether or not the so-called problem of incest will become of apparent importance. Another comparison: the occasional cases of real incest are of as little importance for the ethnic incest prohibitions as the occasional outbursts of bestiality among primitives are for the ancient animal cults. In my opinion the incest barrier can no more be explained by reduction to the possibility of real incest than the animal cult can be explained by reduction to real bestiality. The animal cult is explained by an infinitely long psychological development which is of paramount importance and not by primitive bestial tendencies — these are nothing but the quarry that provides the material for building a temple. But the temple and its meaning have nothing to do with the quality of the building stones. This applies also to the incest taboo, which as a special psychological institution has a much greater — and different — significance than the prevention of incest, even though it may look the same from the outside. (The temple is white, yellow, or red according to the material used.) Like the stones of a temple, the incest taboo is the symbol or vehicle of a far wider and special meaning which has as little to do with real incest as hysteria with the sexual trauma, the animal cult with the bestial tendency and the temple with the stone (or better still, with the primitive dwelling from whose form it is derived). (FJL 505f)

It is important to note that this letter, written in May of 1912, responds to the publication of the first two chapters of *Totem and Taboo* (FJL 502). Freud, in his reply, only acknowledged his previous "error" in confusing dreams of sexual trauma with actual events.

Jung attacks Freud on all fronts, but the crucial idea in the letter is fairly simple: the function of incest barriers is not the prohibition on desire—indeed, desire seems to be left out of consideration altogether—but the constitution of something which, in the structure of the psyche, has nothing to do with sexuality. Here we find an early and relatively clear expression of Jung's view of the function of the symbol. It is not merely a sign for something. Nor is it merely a symptom. Rather, it carries the meaning necessary for transcending the circumstances of the individual at the moment of its expression.

An aspect of the letter which is easily overlooked, in this regard, is the role Jung attributes to regressive reactivation. What Jung is holding out as a bold conjecture is the notion that the course of regression is the source of the symbol, the meaning of which is "far wider and special" than its mere sexual interpretation. This notion harks back to his theory of the teleological nature of the psyche and foreshadows an argument that is essential to understanding Jung, and particularly the central function he attributes to projection, in which libido is seen to purposely regress to earlier levels of experience in order to find the appropriate symbol for further progression. This is a decisive departure from Freud's point of view where the sign is essentially a symptom and does not provide information that is constructive except in the therapeutic setting under the guidance of the analyst who discerns its true significance within a hermeneutics of suspicion.

Shortly after this exchange, Jung traveled to the United States and lectured on the theory of libido as he had come to see it. Upon his return he wrote to Freud of his great success, which was due to the modifications of the theory. Freud came to call this Jung's "boast" in the history of the movement, acknowledging that if one took out the more objectionable sexual aspect of libido theory, one was bound to find more acceptance on the part of the opposition (FJL 517). From this point on, the correspondence became increasingly formal and turned away from the personal problems between the two men. In the end, Jung continued on his course, and Freud was forced to look elsewhere for his much sought heir.

Incest and Authority

Our consideration of the correspondence between Freud and Jung is intended to provide a framework within which to carry out our own interpretation of the question of authority in psychoanalysis. The framework is provided by the Oedipus myth, but the very notion of a mythic dimension to the struggle makes metabiography possible. What then are the characteristics of an interpretation for which the dispute over incest can become thematic?

If we indeed have a great mythic drama of authority and incest being worked out between Freud and Jung, wherein one party sets out to kill the other, we still have only half of the mythic system of the original Oedipus drama. What is lacking is an account of the role of the mother. Where, in other words, is the female side of the myth? The answer to this question, I suggest, is that the Great Mother which both "father" Freud and "son" Jung want to possess, albeit for different reasons, is the unconscious itself.

Freud's concern for authority may thus be seen as an attempt to legislate the relationship which one may have to the unconscious—if the problem is seen in terms of Freudian theory—while Jung, in his claim that the father does not establish the incest taboo, is asserting the primacy of the unconscious itself and the lack of a legitimate legislator, the father, who may institute a prohibition. The mother, Jung would say, attaches the child to herself by making herself forbidden. The unconscious, because it is that which is hidden, is perceived to be of great value. The issue remains one of authority, but we may now expand the dimensions of that problem by proposing that the feminine counterpart to the authoritarian father is the unconsaous itself. In order to work out the implications of this assertion, we must now begin to interpret Freud's system as itself a representation of the problem of incest.

For Freud the Oedipus complex lies at the foundation of religion, and the analysis of Freud's authority now begins to show the characteristics of an attempt to found a religion in which he would be the principal prophet and lawgiver. To get closer to this argument, which defines the standpoint from which Freud and Jung are conducting their dispute, one may propose the following framework. For Freud, the primal authority or law of the traditional religious God has passed, but the succession to that lawgiving authority has been taken up by Freud himself. The object of legislative prohibition, in turn, is the unconscious, which Freud encountered in his self-analysis and which now defines his unique position in the world. It is Freud's wish, in other words, that he legislate in all matters pertaining to the unconscious. In this context, Jung's contrary view of the basic laws of the psyche — the sexual interpretation of libido and the Freudian interpretation of the Oedipus drama — no longer constitutes a simple empirical deviation. It is an apostasy; Jung is a heretic.

A collateral aspect of Freud's accession to the position of lawgiver can now be seen. It is the question of the granting of grace. The analyst is he who forgives in the absence of God. But to receive this grace one must conform to the law. One must admit the truth of Freud's interpretation of Oedipus. Failure to admit one's sin is to fall from grace; Jung falls.

Jung, on the other hand, does not see himself in the place of the lawgiver in the sense in which Freud does, because he does not legislate the way in which the unconscious must be interpreted. Rather, Jung's Gnostic myth necessarily leads him to associate himself with a God beyond who seeks to overcome the archontic law. This means that the dispute with Freud is not, in Jung's mind, one of accession to the place of lawgiver. Rather, the dispute is over access to grace. Does one come to grace through the law or from outside the law by means of direct participation in the fundamental reality? This is, in religious terms, the antinomian dispute.

In its essence, antinomianism teaches the unique and personal access of the individual to God's grace. No mediation is called for, and once grace is received the externally imposed law ceases to confine the individual. I have already discussed Jung's childhood visions and shown how we can surmise that they probably had validity as psychic events. Their numinous content confirmed Jung's conviction that he had received a unique revelation of God's grace. Freud, on the other hand, wanted to be the unique prophet and lawgiver concerning the unconscious, a position that necessitated his rejection of Jung's Gnostic vision on grounds that it had not been properly subjected to the analysis that would subordinate it to Freud's law. These phantasies or wish patterns are clearly irreconcilable.

Incest and the Way to the Unconscious

The difference between Freud and Jung over the interpretation of incest maps the problem of access to the unconscious, the core of psychoanalytic theory, and thereby maps the controversy over authority—the antinomian debate in psychoanalysis. There is, as we have seen, an anthropological moment in the debate which turns on the primacy of patriarchy versus the primacy of matriarchy. As Freud's anthropological assumptions have gone by the scholarly boards, Lacan and others have attempted to rescue the classical form of the incest interpretation by generalizing it to a triangular pattern of desired object, desiring subject, and prohibition on desire.

Examination of Jung's interpretation of incest, however, demonstrates that the problem of patriarchy versus matriarchy is not incidental to the meaning of incest. In fact, the decision is of central importance because it determines the structure of legitimate authority. Anthropology has little or nothing to do with this because the dispute becomes, at this level, philosophical. In its most radical form the controversy centers on the primordial representation of human existence. It is thus an existential problem with far reaching implications. In the case at hand, Jung's commitment to the primacy of the mother forced him to let go of Freud's definition of the nature of the unconscious, which in turn led to a confrontation with the unconscious which he experienced as resembling a psychosis.

II. Transformations

Jung's Quest for a Myth

In the foreword to the 1950 edition of *Transformations*[1] Jung records his reflections on the origins of the book and the break with Freud it precipitated. As was the case with the autobiography's account of the ocean voyage, this foreword is virtually a copy of remarks Jung had made in 1925 (Jung 1989). He had, in fact, begun rethinking *Transformations* shortly after its completion. "Hardly had I finished the manuscript," Jung writes, "when it struck me what it means to live with a myth and what it means to live without one" (CW 5:page xxiv).[2] To live without a myth is the particular objective of the modern mind, but to be in this mythless state was, for Jung, to be "like one uprooted, having no true link either with the past, or with the ancestral life which continues within him, or yet with contemporary society" (CW 5:page xxiv). Jung found that he had stepped out of the magical circle of myth:

> I was driven to ask myself in all seriousness: "What is the myth you are living?" I found no answer to this question, and had to admit that I was not living with a myth, or even in a myth, but rather in an uncertain cloud of theoretical possibilities which I was beginning to regard with increasing distrust. (CW 5:page xxiv f)

The problem for Jung, therefore, became one of defining the myth within which he did, or could, live:

> So, in the most natural way, I took it upon myself to get to know "my" myth, and I regarded this as the task of tasks. For—so I told myself—how could I, when treating my patients, make allowance for the personal factor, for my personal equation, which is yet so necessary for a knowledge of the other person, if I was unconscious of it. (CW 5:page xxv)

The task of Jung's investigations, after *Transformations*, involved an immersion in his own phantasy world, which led to the encounter with the unconscious and the writing of the *Seven Sermons to the Dead* in 1916. But this course was set in the investigations of myth undertaken in *Transformations*. Given the perspective we have already established on the interpretation of incest, it becomes possible to read *Transformations* as a critique of the Freudian myth and as the foundation for a final expression of Jung's counter-myth which was, up to this point, inarticulate but clearly evident in his appropriation of Freud's investigations. To understand the emergence of the Jungian counter-myth, therefore, we must survey the argument of Jung's decisive text.

The Structure of Transformations

Transformations follows a pattern similar to Freud's study of paranoia in the Schreber case. It is an analysis of the recorded phantasies of an American woman Jung had never met. The first part of the book is an analysis of the phantasies of Miss Frank Miller.[3] This is the part of the book that Freud found least disturbing. In large measure the Miller phantasies draw on American folklore—especially the tale of Hiawatha—for the figures constitutive of a myth of the hero. It is Jung's basic contention, however, that, contrary to Freud, it is through the activity of these phantasy images or myths that the libido undergoes successive transformations that lead to a point of view— sometimes termed religious—that may serve to mitigate the onset of psychosis. In this Jung worked out, in a more sophisticated form, the argument he had developed in his dissertation concerning the teleology of the psyche.

Part two of the study, which so greatly upset Freud, is by far the larger portion, and it is this section that deals specifically with the idea of the transformation of libido. A review of the chapter titles alone reveals why Freud reacted as he did. Following an introduction, Jung addresses in turn, "The Concept of the Libido," "The Transformation of Libido," "The Origin of the Hero," "Symbols of the Mother and Rebirth," and "The Sacrifice." It is in this last section that Jung took up his discussion of the nature of incest, and in developing the theme of the sacrifice he worked out an interpretation of the myth of Oedipus that Freud had to reject. Indeed, in his autobiography Jung outlines the tremendous importance he attached to the writing of this section:

> When I was working on my book about the libido and approaching the end of the chapter "The Sacrifice," I knew in advance that its publication would cost me my friendship with Freud. For I planned to set down in it my own conception of libido, and various other ideas in which I differed from Freud. To me incest signified a personal complication only in the rarest cases. Usually incest has a highly religious aspect, for which reason the incest theme plays a decisive part in almost all cosmogonies and in numerous myths. But Freud clung to the literal interpretation of it and could not grasp the spiritual significance of incest as a symbol. I knew that he would never be able to accept any of my ideas on this subject. (MDR 167)

The Object of the Interior World

We have already seen that Freud's conception of the Oedipus complex, and in fact of the incest motif in general, required an analysis of the fundamental mode of relation to the object. Indeed, it is Freud's contention that the incest motif defines the mode of any future object choice. Jung's analysis is similar, with the exception that, in the search for an object of love, the schizophrenic constitutes an interior world where the object may be found. As with Freud, Jung conceives of this search for the object of desire as a crisis in the person's ability to love. In the course of Miss Miller's phantasies, for example, she comes to constitute an elaborate "hypnogogic drama" concerning the hero Chiwantopel. This tale of the trial of a hero becomes her interior world and leads her further away from the world outside her psyche. Jung notes that this form of phantasy bears a striking resemblance to the somnambulistic experiences of mediums where there is a willingness to listen to the inner voice. He then hypothesizes that our inner listening reflects an inward flow of the libido towards an unknown goal (CW5:253). Again, this clearly recalls the notion of teleology Jung proposed in his dissertation. Evidently there is an object that exercises "a powerful attraction" for the subject (CW 5:253). This inward flow in search of the object of attraction, which is particularly acute in the psychotic, brings Jung to a central aspect of his analysis. It is not the lack of external objects that prompts the interior turn but "an inability to love which robs a person" of the opportunity to find an object outside of the psyche (CW 5:253). What would cause such an inability to love? Jung finds that only some resistance "which opposes its obstinate 'won't' to the 'will' is capable of producing a regression that may become the starting point for a pathogenic disturbance" (CW 5:253). In some sense, therefore, psychosis originates in a prohibition; specifically a prohibition on the selection of an object of love. Thus Jung's analysis of psychosis begins with the precise problem which he confronted in Freud, the problem of prohibition.

Psychoanalysis as Myth

Jung notes that in Freud's view the libido can regress to the images of the parents under the pressure of its inherent inertia or unwillingness to relinquish an object of the past (CW 5:253). For Freud, however, "libido" designates the sexual; therefore, any image which presents itself in the event of regression must signify a sexual state of affairs.

This is clearly in keeping with the Lacanian interpretation of Freud which identifies the most primordial contents of the system Ucs with the phallus. Reductive analysis is intent on seeking out this male sexual core of the image in order to release the regressed libido. For Jung, however, the purely sexual understanding of libido is largely a product of adult life (CW 5:299) and is not present in the infant. In other words, Jung rejects infantile sexuality and replaces it with a notion of nutritional instincts or simply an instinct to live. The rejection of the purely sexual theory of desire expands libido theory "into a conception of intentionality [*Intendieren*] in general" (CW 5:197). "We should be better advised, therefore," Jung continues,

> when speaking of libido, to understand it as an energy value which is able to communicate itself to any field of activity whatsoever, be it power, hunger, hatred, sexuality, or religion, without ever being itself a specific instinct. As Schopenhauer says: "The Will as a thing-in-itself is quite different from its phenomenal manifestation and entirely free from all forms of phenomenality, which it assumes only when it becomes manifest, and which therefore affect its objectivity only and are foreign to the Will itself." (CW 5:197)

This passage recalls our treatment of instinct as an analogue of the Kantian thing-in-itself. Jung now uses philosophical commentary to introduce a more complex argument that calls into question the systematic connection between the instinct and its representation. For Jung, even the primordial image of the phallus is ambiguous, as we have seen from his account of his childhood dreams, in that it is the voice of the mother that must be interpreted to give the dream meaning. He argues that the representation of libido may emerge from any of a number of sources and represent a variety of psychic interests. This means that the sexual representation of libido fulfills some fundamental objective in Freud's system. It is not the only possible representation of primordial reality. Arising out of this argument is the notion that the Freudian system itself is, in effect, a set of symbols that make up a myth. The result is that Freud's system is itself as susceptible to the techniques of myth analysis as is the Gilgamesh epic.

The Analysis of Myth: The Sphinx

If we now turn to myth proper, as Freud had done in his attempt to vindicate the sexual theory of the libido, we must dramatically complicate our interpretation, according to Jung. We must pay attention to all of the details of the myth rather than simply to some alleged core motif. In the case of Oedipus, Jung first of all undertakes to interpret the meaning of the Sphinx and immediately comes upon the fact that this strange creature is itself the result of an incestuous union between mother and son and, like Oedipus, a product of birth out of the Earth, making her, in effect, Oedipus's cousin (CW 5:265). The Sphinx's femininity also involves it in the motif of Oedipus's confrontation with the female world, the world of the mother. The Sphinx is, in fact, a "semi-theriomorphic representation of the mother-imago or rather the Terrible Mother, who has left numerous traces in mythology" (CW 5:261). Since the Sphinx has also been sent to Thebes by another aspect of the Great Mother, Hera, the riddling of the Sphinx, Jung argues, must have a meaning beyond the rather simple conundrum which it indeed puts to male passersby. On Jung's reading of the myth "the riddle of the Sphinx was herself — the terrible mother-imago, which Oedipus would not take as a warning" (CW 5:265). What we find in the Oedipus myth, therefore, is a succession of incestuous situations, tied to the Great Mother, not all of which involve a desire for intercourse with the mother in any conventional sense. Oedipus is only thrice removed from birth out of the earth, the ultimate form of the Great Mother, and it is in his return to the earth, itself an incest motif, in the sanctuary of the Erinyes who, transformed into the Eumenides ("gracious ones," MR 183), protect mothers, that he finally achieves his rest, having been guided there by Antigone, the pure representation of incest. Jung also notes that in the two incestuous encounters that precede his death, the female participant — the Sphinx and Jocasta — meet death, while Oedipus is increased in wisdom and holiness. Clearly, an extremely complex interpretation is needed if all of the elements of the myth are to be accounted for.

The sense of complexity in Oedipus is symbolized by the very notion of riddling. What deeper sense can we find in the riddle? Not only does the Sphinx put a question to Oedipus, the action of the play itself begins with another riddle, the source of the plague. The encounter with the mother-imago, therefore, seems to involve finding a solution to a problem. Kerenyi suggests that the riddle of the Sphinx is not dissimilar to the Delphic injunction, "know thyself," and that the constant recurrence of Delphi in the story adds an important dimension to this interpretation (Kerenyi 1978:98). We will not digress into the mythology of Delphi at this time other than to note that its original patron was Gaia, the earth (Guthrie 1955:80), which again leaves us with a strong sense of just how involved the interpretation of this myth can be where the question of the Great Mother is concerned.

Interpretation of the Great Mother

This is not to say that Freud could not accommodate the problem of the mother had he altered his theory. But there is an inadequacy in Freud's theory that rests on the necessity to subordinate the mother to the action taking place between father and son. (Even in the case of Leonardo, there is a phallo-centrism at work in the interpretation of the role of the mother.(SE XI:97).) Freud must hold fast to the argument that this subordination gives us the definitive interpretation of the myth, and that the many layers of Great Mother imagery are either a late addition to the myth or, more likely, an unconscious subterfuge. This argument simply fails, however, in terms of giving an interpretation of the myth. I must emphasize that I am not arguing for the transparency of the manifest form of the myth. To the contrary. But Freud takes the step of finding in ancient sources the proof texts for his theories, and my claim, with Jung, is that Freud fails to examine thoroughly the texts which he has selected, and this for ideological reasons that are tied to the problem of authority in psychoanalysis.

If Jung is correct, on the other hand, the Sphinx presents Oedipus with a prospective vision of his own being by posing the riddle which she is, herself, in her own being. The problem that Oedipus has to solve in every one of the riddles or decisions he confronts is the problem of the return to the mother. The injunction to know oneself is thus a call to return to origins, and Oedipus is the primal actor in this drama because he eventually returns to the earth after having passed through several prior encounters with the mother. Here we must note that it is only Oedipus who can overcome one case of incest, the Sphinx, in order to enter into a more profound case of incest. Oedipus's self-blinding leads to a deep inward turn following upon the successive encounters with incest which end, to repeat, in his return to the primal mother, the earth.

Regression: The Return to the Mother

As with Freud, regression for Jung implies a return to unconscious contents of the psyche. But Jung goes a step further by proposing a reason for the negative valuation usually given to regressive behavior. The problem with regression is that it begins to yield the most terrible images at a fairly early stage due to the stimulation of the instinctual level of being. According to Jung, the regression sets in, in the first place, because of a failure of adaptation (CW 5:506). And this failure of adaptation results in the return of consciousness to its primal foundations in the unconscious. It is at this point that the unconscious, in the form of the mother, becomes a source of terror (CW 5:457).

This notion allows us to begin to vindicate the earlier claim that the seat of the dispute between Freud and Jung was itself Oedipal, in the sense developed here, in that it involved a conflict over possession of the mother seen as the unconscious. The issue is this: the conflict between Freud and Jung is itself a representation of the Oedipus drama and, therefore, alternative interpretations of the incest motif constitute alternative interpretations of the conflict between the two men.

We have already seen that Freud at first welcomed Jung's insight into the persistence of myth motifs in psychic activity. Freud, however, wanted to see the myth as a sign of regressive activity in the psyche, while Jung conceived of the myth as a guide for the psyche in its search for meaning. The myth is a symbol, for Jung, in that it is forward looking; it projects into the future even as it points back to problems in the past. Thus the incestuous return to the mother is the symbol for the recovery of libido to its point of origin from which a new birth can take place. "When the libido leaves the bright upperworld," Jung writes, whether from choice, or from inertia, or from fate, it sinks back into its own depths, into the source from which it originally flowed, and returns to the point of cleavage, the navel, where it first entered the body. This point of cleavage is called the mother, because from her the current of life reached us. Whenever some great work is to be accomplished, before which a man recoils, doubtful of his strength, his libido streams back to the fountainhead — and that is the dangerous moment when the issue hangs between annihilation and a new life. For if the libido gets stuck in the wonderland of this inner world, then for the upperworld man is nothing but a shadow, he is already moribund or at least seriously ill. But if the libido manages to tear itself loose and force its way up again, something like a miracle happens: the journey to the underworld was a plunge into the fountain of youth, and the libido, apparently dead, wakes to renewed fruitfulness. (CW 5:449)

It is precisely in the tendency to become stuck fast in the underworld — in a psychosis — that Freud finds the need for society to defend itself against the incestuous introversion of libido. Jung is aware of this position, but he would also see a danger in any failure to accommodate the demands of the unconscious.[4]

The Death of the Mother and the Birth of the Hero

Let us now apply this interpretation of the mother to the myth of Oedipus itself. What is implicit in Jung's interpretation, first of all, is a deepening of the meaning which we can attach to the Sphinx. She is an expression of the Great Mother and an expression of incest, but she is also a monster that Oedipus must overcome. This makes the Sphinx an anticipatory projection of that part of the life of Oedipus which works itself out in his eventual overcoming of the regression of incest and the subsequent emergence of progressive levels of consciousness, first in the form of the hero of Thebes and then in the form of the semi-divine guarantor of Athens. In both cases of the emergence of the higher form of consciousness on the part of Oedipus, however, it is necessary that the imago of the mother — first the Sphinx and then Jocasta — commit suicide. In other words, the emergence of the hero demands the overcoming of an image of the mother, an event that Jung interprets as a relinquishing of containment within the unconscious (CW5:415), but which also points to the integration of the unconscious feminine, which Jung would later call the anima, into the psyche of the male. A corresponding process may readily be posited for the woman, with Antigone as a likely paradigm in place of Oedipus.

This is by no means the only movement in the dialectic of the myth, however. There remains the counter-sacrifice of the father and the son. Jung never rejected the notion that one moment in the drama of Oedipus was the killing of the father. He might have interpreted it differently from Freud but he did not ignore it. Freud, on the other hand, is willing to make much of the killing of the father and even of the event which corresponds in time to Jocasta's death, Oedipus's self-blinding as symbolic self-castration, but he ignores the suicide of Jocasta. It appears that he does this for two reasons. One is personal, involving Freud's intense relationship to his own mother. The other is systematic and again brings us to the problem of authority, which now can be seen to devolve on the interpretation of the myth of the hero, that is, the myth of the self-sufficient man.

It would be a mistake to conceive of the hero as a hypermasculine personality. In Jung's terms, the hero is he who has successfully incorporated the unconscious into himself in other words, the hero must incorporate the feminine rather than resist it.[5] If this integration of the personality is to be achieved, then it is precisely the resistance to entry into the unconscious which must be overcome. This may take the form of the killing of the father, but now Jung gives another sense to that act by interpreting it in light of what will be termed the primacy of projection. The killing of the father becomes the withdrawal of the projection, the overcoming of a part of oneself.[6] Given our earlier discussion of the place of the father in the constitution of authority, of the law, in the Freudian *Weltanschauung*, we can now see directly into the response Jung proposes to advance against Freud's conception. The problem centers on the formation of personal symbols of redemption in the son's self-sacrifice to the mother.

Incest and the Origin of Symbols

The incest taboo prohibits a return to the source out of which emerge the fundamental symbols of the social or religious order, that is, mythology. The psyche can be satisfied, for relatively long periods of time, with the mythology deployed within a culture, in which case the incest taboo serves to preserve the established order by insisting on the canalization of libido into established symbol systems (CW 5:313). Jung's example is the divine city which replaces the mother as a representation of libido but is itself, as a symbol, a product of the unconscious—thus Oedipus's relationship first to Thebes and then to Athens. But an established mythology cannot simply ignore the regressive incest impulse, the attractive power of the unconscious, once it has been prohibited. And so the impulse is itself transferred into the rite of the mythology. The god figure in the mythology is allowed to achieve the union with the mother which is denied to everyone else. In antiquity and later in Christianity this was the function of the *heiros gamos*, the divine marriage. The mystical sense of the cross in medieval Christianity can be interpreted "as the *heiros gamos* of the god with his mother for the purpose of conquering death and renewing life" (CW 5:411). In its essence, Jung argues, the *heiros gamos* is an opportunity for man to participate in incest without practicing incest.

It would seem that this practice of the religious rite fits perfectly into a Freudian pattern of substitution; it is merely a displacement. This argument, however, turns decisively against Freud in that it requires that an account be given of the larger structure of the Oedipus drama. For example, Oedipus's death is associated, at least in some traditions, with the mysteries of Demeter, the Eleusinian mysteries (cf. Kerenyi 1977:84f). What starts as incest becomes the birth of the divine child, which is itself a myth of the overcoming of death, and the entire drama finally circles around into the most basic sense of fertility. The rebirth motif confirms, it would seem, the primal will to life as the basic form of will or instinct since it is the common denominator in all of the myths.

But we may also argue that the corollary to the prohibition on the exploration of new symbols and the compensatory reenactment of the incest wish in religious ritual is to be found in Freud's benevolent permission for the patient to think out all of the incestuous wishes in the consulting room. To put it another way, Freud's claim to have already in his possession the truth about the role of sexuality in the psyche is tantamount to the constitution of a religious system in which certain rites are allowed in order to mitigate the incest wish in such a way that it is impossible for an alternative symbolism to emerge.

At the same time, Freud himself assumes the position of the one who does in fact achieve union with the mother by way of a heroic self-sacrifice. Freud alone knows the mysteries of the unconscious. One may come to the unconscious only by way of Freud. Here we encounter the essential assertion of authority in psychoanalysis; Freud's analytic program rests on a prohibition against any other encounter with the mother. Anyone who attempts to reach the unconscious must do so, in Freud's myth, by killing him. But the key to the system is that it is precisely in killing the father that the taboo on access to the mother becomes inviolate. Freud's desire for death at the hands of his most gifted followers is thus an expression of his desire to confirm his system of authority.

Jung's Response to Authority: Psychological Cosmogony

We may conclude this discussion of incest by outlining Jung's response to Freud's attempt to assert the primacy of his approach to the unconscious. Formulated in terms of a philosophy of mythology and a theory of authority, the establishment of a myth, in this case the myth of psychoanalysis, is in fact an extremely powerful move to make in the cultural economics of an age. One does not simply bypass a genuine myth and propose an alternative, and there is no question that Freud sets up a genuine myth with all its powerful self-regulating agencies. This means that Jung is in fact prevented from merely proposing an alternative psychology of the unconscious because Freud's vision is in fact a profound mythic expression of the unconscious. The answer to the prohibitions, the claims to authority, set up by Freud must, therefore, lie in another direction. That answer, for Jung, requires entry into his own encounter with the unconscious, an encounter which he experienced as being similar to a psychosis. We have already seen how Jung's early work focused on the psychotic; it was precisely his attempt to account for the loss of reality in psychosis that led him to alter the theory of the libido. In *Transformations,* the nature of psychosis remains central, and Jung argues that the symbolism of the incest motif moves, in the last analysis, to myth motifs suitable for an interpretation of the psychotic loss of reality in the myths of the great cosmogonic sacrifices. This movement leads to the deepest stratum in the philosophical consideration of psychoanalytic theory where we must ask about the basic nature of reality and its relationship to time.

Jung approaches this problem in *Transformations* from the point of view of the desire to overcome time and solve the riddle of death. When this cannot be accomplished in the world of consciousness or sense experience, a world of phantasy appears from the unconscious and offers a route of advance. At this point, however, unconscious and conscious confront one another in the creation of symbols. In its prohibition on the formation of any new symbolism of the unconscious, Freud's psychoanalysis is fundamentally incapable of solving the problem of death and time. Jung, on the other hand, is drawn by this problem to a consideration of the great myths of world constitution and world renunciation: the sacrifice of containment in the mother and the sacrifice of the world to the mother, the sacrifice of return.

The first sacrifice results in a "psychological cosmogony." The incest taboo, in this instance, serves to reveal the world previously hidden in unconsciousness:

> The world comes into being when man discovers it. But he only discovers it when he sacrifices his containment in the primal mother, the original state of unconsciousness. What drives him towards this discovery is conceived by Freud as the "incest barrier." (CW 5:652)

Seen now as part of a cosmogonic myth, incest leads on to successive movements of libido, always seeking higher levels of expression. Thus once the world is constituted it may also be renounced. A symbolic representation of this is the mythic horse sacrifice:

> [T]he horse-sacrifice signifies a renunciation of the world. When the horse is sacrificed the world is sacrificed and destroyed . . . . The horse stands between two vessels, passing from one to the other, just as the sun passes from morning to evening. Since the horse is man's steed and works for him . . . the horse signifies a quantum of energy that stands at man's disposal. It therefore represents the libido which has passed into the world. We saw earlier on that the "mother libido" must be sacrificed in order to create the world; here the world is destroyed by renewed sacrifice of the same libido, which once belonged to the mother and then passed into the world. The horse,

therefore, may reasonably be substituted as a symbol for this libido because . . . It has numerous connections with the mother. The sacrifice of the horse can only produce another phase of introversion similar to that which prevailed before the creation of the world. (CW 5:658f)

These progressive symbolic acts are directed precisely at the problem of time in the sense of the confrontation with death, for it is by means of sacrifice that "man ransoms himself from the fear of death and is reconciled to the demands of the destroying mother" (CW5:671). This double movement in the mythology of sacrifice places us on the threshold of an understanding of the loss of reality in psychosis as a dialectical moment in Jung's confrontation with Freud's authority. The crucial idea here is the hero's self-sacrifice to the mother, the unconscious. Just as Oedipus blinds himself and finally finds rest in his return to the earth, his primordial place of origin, so the hero must regenerate himself through "his self-sacrifice and reentry into the mother" (CW 5:671). This leads to an overcoming of the problem of death—the crucifixtion comes to be seen as "a *heiros gamos* with the mother" (CW 5:671).

This is precisely the undertaking that confronted Jung after the break with Freud, and it became, as he emerged from his encounter with the unconscious, the source of a new interpretation of the psyche. But there is a deeper stratum of significance here as well. We have seen that killing becomes the source of authority in Freud's interpretation of incest. The problem which we confronted at that juncture was the denial of natural death within culture and the primacy of killing as the only possible experience of death in civilization. Jung now proposes an alternative and thereby seeks to overturn the system of authority deployed by Freud. The alternative is self-sacrifice. Thus, rather than allow himself to be drawn into Freud's drama by acting out the killing of the father, it is Jung himself who must undertake a voluntary death, by way of his own renunciation of the world, and turn to the unconscious itself.

With this we come to a crucial juncture in the development of a theory of authority. Death dominates the analysis. But the primacy of death engages us in the problem of the existential relationship to time. We have already seen how the argument for the primal killing entails a retrospective comprehension of death. The primacy of killing means that the death that really matters is in the past. One's own death, in the future, is meaningless. This points to a particular form of constraint on the experience of time, and we will now see how it is that the domination of time becomes, by way of myth, the essence of Freud's system of authority. Indeed, the structure of this conception of authority carries with it certain claims about time and the timeless which will deepen our understanding of incest and the philosophical dimensions of Jung's struggle with Freud.

Six

Time and Psyche

Time and Psychoanalysis

The claim that the problem of death brings time to the fore also unifies the philosophical analysis of Jung's struggle with Freud. We have already seen in some detail how temporality is decisive for understanding in psychoanalysis. Thus we can interpret Jung's first work of psychological investigation, his dissertation, as a study in the psychology of time insofar as Helene, the medium, retreats to a primordial or "timeless" state to find the authoritative image for her developmental progress. What is more important, we find in this encounter the teleological shaping of Jung's own life project as a psychologist as he observes, by way of the medium, the primordial, timeless world of the unconscious in the figure of the Great Mother, Ivenes. Psychological retrospection gives way to practical prospection as the project of Jung's career emerges in the seances. It must be added, however, that Jung undertakes this developmental project only after breaking the spell of the unconscious expression by revealing the medium's fabrication of the voices.

A similar theme is at work in the problem that we now see dominating the drama of psychoanalysis itself, the interpretation of incest. The crucial claim is that Freud's interpretation places the death of the father by the murderous sons at the center of psychoanalytic meaning. By way of my analysis of the significance of this claim, I have attempted to show that this locates the most important moment of existential self-understanding in the past. I no longer anticipate my own death, in a world where Freud's interpretation of incest is dominant, because my self-understanding is tied to an image of killing located in a primordial past to which I have no self-evident means of access. Access is prohibited by an analysis of incest wherein prohibition and guilt lie at the center of culture. All of this results in a closure of the unconscious that places Freud's system of interpretation at the starting point of any attempt at self-understanding. This entire system of meaning, therefore, may be called Freud's metabiographical delimitation of biographical self-consciousness. Metabiography, we now begin to see, is an essential element of Freud's authority in that existential self-consciousness can be brought under a set of categories that derive from an interpretation of his radical encounter with the unconscious in his self-analysis. Underlying this level of understanding, however, is the level of the primal psychic mechanisms that give rise to the representation of instincts in the first place. We examined repression in chapter four and we will take up projection in chapter seven. What must be said on both topics at this point is that the decision concerning which of them is the constitutive mechanism of the psyche lies at the heart of the metabiographical enterprise because it determines the temporal orientation of interpretation and self-consciousness. Thus we have already seen that repression must be the presupposition of Freud's retrospective reconstruction of the Oedipus drama. We will see, in chapter seven, that projection is the functional presupposition of Jung's prospective program of interpretation.

What we must grasp in the present chapter is the notion that Freud and Jung are at variance with one another on the issue of the temporal role of the unconscious. This is a basic level of understanding in our effort to comprehend the conflict between the two men, and it shapes subsequent attempts to bring their respective systems to bear on the interpretation of both psychological and cultural phenomena.

Internally, the argument of this chapter will draw, first, on a consideration of Freud's vision of the timelessness of the unconscious. I will then show that Freud's attention to language, in preference to the image, reflects his predisposition concerning time in that the decision concerning the primacy of language and the subordination of image is an expression of Freud's entire retrospective enterprise. Then, by recourse to a consideration of Nietzsche, I will show that the retrospective construction of meaning has important consequences for our understanding of the problem of authority and Freud's role as the primal patriarch of psychoanalysis.

This last point is nested in a larger cultural issue that can only be elaborated as we take up time and meaning in the context of the reinterpretation of incest undertaken in Jung and outlined in the second section of chapter five. There we began to consider the problem of the loss and recovery of the world in the movement of consciousness between encounters with the unconscious and the world of action: the sacrifice to the mother and the sacrifice of the mother. In less mythic terms, we may call this the loss of reality and meaning in the encounter with the unconscious followed by their recovery in a return to the world of action. For purposes of the present discussion we may introduce this problem of the recovery of meaning by asking the following question: Why should a profound metabiographical enterprise such a Freud's be undertaken, with such epochal consequences, at the time it was? This question reflects a concern for the conditions that underlie the emergence of new systems of meaning and their relevance to self-consciousness.

The Boundaries of Time

The rubric under which I will discuss the issue of time and meaning will be the "boundaries of time," which is premised on the possibility of interpreting the temporal significance of myths in one of two ways: myths may be subject to time and rise and fall with the passage of time; or myths may define the comprehension of human historical time by giving us, for example, an age of Christendom. In the first interpretation time sets boundaries to meaning, insofar as meaning is given in a viable myth. In the second instance meaning, as given by the myth, sets boundaries on our sense of time in that the loss of the myth's interpretative power is taken to be symbolic of the end of time. I have put forward the idea that a dispute over meaning and access to meaning was at the center of the crisis of authority in Jung's struggle with Freud. If we now link meaning to time by way of myth we will find, as I suggested, that authority and time are inextricably bound up with one another. Indeed, a dialectic of authority will emerge from a consideration of the double movement of myth and meaning in relation to the boundaries of time, this double movement being implicit in the two interpretative options just outlined. The problem of meaning and time will bring us, in turn, to a deeper understanding of the drama of psychoanalysis in a confrontation with phenomena that both Jung and Freud considered to be frighteningly similar, in form, to the collapse into psychosis. To begin to make sense of this argument, and to give content to the notion of the boundaries of time, let us turn briefly to Jung's view of a historical age.

The Concept of an Age

As we have seen, for Jung the solution to a crisis of self-understanding grows out of the reconciliation of psychic experience to a definitive myth that provides a context for ongoing acts of interpretation. But this definitive myth must bear a relationship to time. Ultimately it must define a historical period either for an individual or for a collectivity. The most familiar example of such a myth is that of the Christian era. To the degree that the mythology of Christianity continues to be historically viable, it defines a range of interpretations given to psychic and cultural activity.

Jung's classic example of this function of Christian myth is the life of the fifteenth-century Swiss mystic Nicholas of Flue, "Brother Klaus" (1417–1487), for whom the dogmatic structure of the Christian myth was indispensable for an adequate interpretation of his visions (for Jung's discussion of Brother Klaus, see CW 11:474ff). Without the interpretative power of the doctrine of the Trinity, Jung argues, Brother Klaus, who experienced a great vision in his hermit's cave, would have been left with a purely numinous and thoroughly terrifying experience, with no meaning to it. Indeed, when he was first found in his cave, following his great vision, his face was so distorted with fear that others could not look at him. As it was, three years elapsed before he could satisfactorily communicate the content of his vision. During those years he labored to paint the vision on the wall of his cave and found, in the end, that the Trinity provided the most satisfactory images. There then followed a further cultural elaboration of the visions on the part of the Church that, while making the visions into increasingly complex testaments to dogma, succeeded eventually in reducing to insignificance the original numinous experience. The result of this project of interpretation was at least twofold. On the one hand, recourse to images as a means of interpretation enabled Brother Klaus to avoid an explosion of psychic forces; on the other, the social structure avoided disruption thanks to an act of discursive interpretation by the Church. The strength of the myth may thus be measured by its ability to overcome the threat of an undifferentiated psychic experience. The alternative to the life of Brother Klaus, in Jung's opinion, was represented by Johannes Scheffler (1624–1677), who called himself Angelus Silesius, and who ended his life in insanity, unable to assimilate his psychic experiences because of the collapse of the system of images and dogmatic interpretations during the Reformation (CW 6:433).

The shift in the interpretative power of Christian symbolization between the fifteenth and the seventeenth centuries points to a situation where time sets the boundaries of meaning in a myth. I call this state of affairs the "life cycle" of a myth. What happens, in other words, when a myth has run its course? Jung's examples suggest that when a myth does run its course the interpretation of psychic experience, especially numinous experiences, becomes problematic if not impossible. Meaning has a life expectancy, a limit on its availability to consciousness, established by the life cycle of the myth.

We can clarify this notion by reflecting on the Platonic view of world ages in which the Christian is but one era among many: when time has exhausted the meaning of a mythology, a new system of meaning must present itself. It is at this point in the development of a system of meaning that the issue becomes complicated as we encounter a reversal of the notion of boundary and find that the myth of the age defines time itself. Time is bounded by the interpretative space provided by the myth, and, when the myth ceases to influence meaning, time is said to come to an end. Apocalyptic visions tend to have this quality.

Thus we find that the concept of the boundaries of time is dialectical and that the two options with which we began are interactive with one another. This dialectical interaction influences interpretative projects insofar as in the experience of the collapse of meaning we arrive at a cultural analogue of the experience of a psychosis. Hellenistic antiquity, in the hiatus between the ancient religions and the emergence of a new myth in Christianity, had these characteristics.

Similarly, Freud saw himself setting in motion a new period in human understanding. One expression of this vision, which he used primarily for polemical purposes, was that psychoanalysis was part of the larger cultural project called "science." Freud's investigations, however, and the evidence of the correspondence, point to a much larger framework of self-understanding wherein psychoanalysis resides somewhere in the midst of the collapse of the "world age" of European Christendom. As such, psychoanalysis shares historical space, as Ricoeur has pointed out, with the works of Marx and Nietzsche. This fact creates a number of problems, for we may ask whether psychoanalysis is the last act of the old age or the first act of the new age. What position does psychoanalysis hold in the hiatus between ages and, if a crisis of meaning is characteristic of the hiatus, what is the contribution of psychoanalysis to the end or beginning of meaning? Do we find, in Freud's enterprise, and in Jung's struggle with Freud, any analogue of the profound inward movement of the psychoses to which I compare cultural collapse? To answer these questions we must first examine Freud's technical discussion of the relationship between time and the unconscious.

Timelessness of the Unconscious

Freud's classic formulation of the place of time in his theories appeared in 1915 when he wrote:

> The processes of the system Ucs are timeless, i.e., they are not ordered temporally, are not altered by the passage of time, in fact bear no relationship to time at all. Reference to time is bound up, once again, with the work of the system Cs. (SE XIV: 187)

The timelessness of the unconscious had been a long-standing doctrine for Freud, going back at least as far as 1895 when he raised the problem in relation to the early neurological view of the psyche (SE 1:310). In 1897, in his notes (Draft M), he wrote concerning phantasy that "chronological corrections seem to depend precisely on the activity of the consciousness" (SE 1:252). This claim cuts deeply into the structure of psychoanalysis, for as Ricoeur observes:

> In Freudianism the sense of depth or profundity lies in the temporal dimension, or more exactly, in the connection between the time function of consciousness and the characteristic of timelessness of the unconscious. (FP 442)[1]

The "time function of consciousness" to which Ricoeur refers is the other side of the claim to the timelessness of the unconscious, and the claim persists to the end in Freud. Thus in 1933, Freud tied these ideas to philosophical claims concerning the second topography. In the *New Introductory Lectures* he writes:

> The relationship to time, which is so hard to describe, is also introduced into the ego by the perceptual system; it can scarcely be doubted that the mode of operation of that system is what provides the origin of the idea of time. (SE XXII:76)

Reality-Testing

Freud's discussion in this passage focuses on reality-testing, which he considers to be the foundation of the sense of the ego. He writes, immediately before the quotation just cited, that the essential distinction to be drawn between the ego and the other two parts of the second topography, the id and the superego, lies in the ego's relationship to the "outer most superficial portion of the mental apparatus" (SE XXII:75) which he designates perceptual-consciousness. This relationship is not in itself superficial or insignificant, since it is in its apprehension of the external world that the ego is able to control the id:

> The relationship to the external world has become the decisive factor for the ego; it has taken on the task of representing for the id, which could not escape destruction if, in its blind efforts for the satisfaction of its instincts, it disregarded that supreme external power. In accomplishing this function, the ego must observe the external world, must lay down an accurate picture of it in the memory-traces of its perceptions, and by its exercise of the function of 'reality-testing' must put aside whatever in this picture of the external world is an addition derived from internal sources of excitation. (SE XXII:75)

The interesting problem with reality-testing is that its consideration of time cannot be subsumed under the more conventional view of the testing process that involves simple motor control of the environment (LP 384). If time, as a restraint on desire, was simply a matter of motor control, then we could ascribe the same form of ego consciousness to the lower animals as to humans since we may readily observe an animal's sense of when to act and when not to. But, according to Freud's myth of the primal horde, ego-consciousness is a relatively late arrival on the scene, and mere timing, therefore, is not the issue in controlling the instincts. By associating the ego's sense of time with the primal killing, however, we begin to see the foundations of Freud's system in an analysis of the time of founding itself. To put it another way, the reality of the psychic topography is a product of the reality of repression, just as the reality of one's psychic state is tied to the temporal experience of the past. One may test the reality of a physiological neurosis by way of motor control. Temporal distortion, however, is far more complex.

The issue will begin to show more sense if we turn to what Freud would call a neurotic desire to transcend time, either by living forever or by actually escaping from time. Then, insofar as the desire to escape from time assumes the dimensions of a religious impulse, we will see that one aspect of Freud's analysis of the relationship to time is a concern for reality testing as a means to provide guarantees for the role of reason (SE XXII:33).

Reality and Projection

In "Metapsychological Supplement to the Theory of Dreams" (1917), Freud writes that "we shall place reality testing among the major institutions of the ego, alongside the censorships which we have come to recognize between the psychical systems" (SE XIV:233). Given the strength of this pronouncement, we can easily see that any assault on the process of reality-testing must necessarily become an assault on the integrity of the ego. But the assault on the ego would originate from within, from the uncontrolled demands of the instincts. In "The Instincts and Their Vicissitudes" (1915) Freud defined the role played by the initial encounter with the external world as that of distinguishing the instincts from other mental stimuli. On the side of the outer stimuli the "apperceptive substance of the living organism" determines that it can interact successfully with the world by recourse to motor activity while the inner experience of instinct cannot be successfully dealt with in this manner (SE XIV:119). This process of discovery has an outcome that goes beyond mere orientation. The psychic subject discovers that those experiences that comprise the external world can be effectively dealt with, especially when they are threatening. A wish-structure now emerges which seeks to deal with the demands of the instincts in the same manner. Projection is born.

> It is of value to the individual to possess a means such as this of recognizing reality, which at the same time helps him to deal with it, and he would be glad to be equipped with a similar weapon against the often merciless claims of his instincts. That is why he takes such pains to transpose outwards what becomes troublesome to him from within — that is, to project it. (SE XIV:233)

By way of this process, neurotic phantasies are reproduced in the world. They attach themselves to objects in the world, and reality-testing becomes the means of overcoming such projections of inner conflict. But at the same time, reality-testing reveals the products of the unconscious to be essentially wish oriented in nature and activity. This characteristic of projection, in Freud's system, is identical with his definition of dreams — they are devices for wish-fulfillment — and, indeed, we find that dreams are a form of projection, an externalization of an internal threat to sleep (SE XIV:233). With this we come to the true venue of Freudian interpretation. The dream, as the royal way to the unconscious, is the hallmark of Freud's system of interpretation. And in the characteristics of dream interpretation we find that Freud's theory of meaning rests on the distinction between word and image.

Word and Image

Sleep, according to Freud, is an extreme form of narcissism in that it represents "a withdrawal of cathexis from all ideas of objects, both from the unconscious and preconscious portions of those ideas" (SE XIV:224). There nevertheless remains in the unconscious a set of memory traces of things encountered during the day that come to form the manifest content of the dream and disrupt sleep. When instinctual activity settles on these traces of things, the traces begin to fill the ideational requirements of the unconscious.

> In this process thoughts are transformed into images, mainly of a visual sort; that is to say word-presentations are taken back to the

thing-presentations which correspond to them, as if, in general, the process were dominated by considerations of representability. (SE XIV:228)

It is at this level that systematic distortion of communication comes into play. Freud hypothesizes that it is by recourse to images that the unconscious contrives to overcome the censorship. The image succeeds where the word does not. Its success in deceiving the censorship serves, in Freud's analysis, to confirm his contention that the essential structures of the psyche center on the linguistic rather than the imagistic.[2] The rearrangement of the linguistic becomes the purpose of the dream. The goal of the *Traumarbeit*, as Freud states, is precisely the remarkable rearrangement of the verbal required to achieve the plastic representation of the dream (SE XIV:228). The importance of this conception of the dream for a theory of meaning cannot be overemphasized, for it is precisely at this point "that the essential difference between the dream-work and schizophrenia becomes clear" (SE XIV:229). Freud continues:

> In the latter, what becomes the subject of modification by the primary process are the words themselves in which the preconscious thought was expressed; in dreams, what are subject to this modification are not the words, but the thing-presentations to which the words have been taken back. In dreams there is a topographical regression; in schizophrenia there is not. In dreams there is free communication between (Pcs.) word-cathexis and (Ucs.) thing-cathexis, while it is characteristic of schizophrenia that this communication is cut off. The impression this difference makes on one is lessened precisely by the dream-interpretations we carry out in psycho-analytic practice. For, owing to the fact that dream-interpretation traces the course taken by the dream-work, follows the paths which lead from the latent thoughts to the dream elements, reveals the way in which verbal ambiguities have been exploited, and points out the verbal bridges between different groups of material—owing to all this, we get an impression now of a joke, now of schizophrenia, and are apt to forget that for a dream all operations with words are no more than a preparation for a regression to things. (SE XIV:229)

In the nonpsychotic person, primary process directs the attention of the psyche to representations of satisfaction realized in the past. It is, in other words, a process of temporal regression that seeks "to reestablish the situation of the original satisfaction" (SE V:565). This movement to the perception of the fulfillment of the wish is the shortest path to satisfaction, but it is not the path taught by reality (FP 108). It is, rather, the timelessness of the unconscious that makes rapid regression to the image of satisfaction possible, and it is the image-bound structure of the unconscious that satisfies perception in the dream state. The higher levels of the psyche, those closer to reality, on the other hand, are language oriented. However, in schizophrenia, when language becomes the object of fixation, and therefore subject to the imperatives of the unconscious, communication with reality breaks down.

We begin to grasp the significance of this problem by recalling Rieff's characterization of Freud's psychoanalysis as a devotion to talk, which thematizes Freud's concern for the "free communication between systems." This is at the heart of the economics of the psyche and forms the basis of the therapeutic method. The analyst, Freud maintains, must be able to move with critical insight between the systems of the psyche, from the images of the system Ucs to the verbal translations of those images in the systems Pcs and Cs This movement reflects Freud's general presupposition of the primacy of the linguistic, even in the organization of the images of the Ucs As Ricoeur observes, this

> linguistic interpretation has the merit of raising the phenomena of primary process and repression to the rank of language; the very fact that the analytic cure itself is a process dependent on language attests to the mixture of the quasi language of the unconscious and ordinary language. (FP 405)

Failure to effect the transitions among the various languagelike domains, however, results in continuation of a hallucinatory state directed toward the language of the dream itself, a state of affairs which Freud considers remarkably similar to schizophrenia. The reason for this lies in the fact that the schizophrenic attaches, according to Freud, a hypercathexis to the word rather than to the object. The result of this process of withdrawal from the object in favor of the word is the re-establishment of "a primitive objectless condition of narcissism" (SE XIV:197) which in turn results in an inability of the patient to achieve the transference necessary for therapy. In the transference, repression acts specifically on the association of words suited to the therapeutic activity with their appropriate unconscious ideas

(SE XIV:201). In schizophrenia the words come to dominate to such an extent that therapy is impossible. This leads to the consideration that the process of repression at work in schizophrenia may indeed be altogether different from that at work in transference neurosis (SE XIV:203). The schizophrenic, Freud concludes, "treats concrete things as though they were abstract" (SE XIV:204). This move, on the part of the schizophrenic, results in the generally accepted characterization of the psychosis wherein the patient withdraws from reality (Bleuler, 1950:378).

The Loss of Time: Schizophrenia

What is lacking in the schizophrenic, in other words, is that essential institution of the ego, reality-testing. Using the language of the first topography, schizophrenia is, in a sense, a collapse of the systems Pcs. and Cs into the system Ucs. While in the neuroses there is an active attachment to some object in the outer world that serves to guide the neurotic in his behavior, the psychotic replaces the external world with an internal phantasy world. The world of phantasy thus replaces the world of reality. If we now recall Freud's claim that the idea of time is introduced by the perceptual system, we may clearly see that the logic of the withdrawal from reality in the psychotic implies a withdrawal from time. This engages us, again, in philosophical considerations. The notion of the loss of time due to a retreat from reality is tied to the concept of the boundaries of time discussed above and to the question of how images for the organization of the psyche are deployed during a crisis of meaning.

The issue that I raise at this point is the following: Jung's analysis of the two mystics, briefly outlined above, points to the notion that the organization of a numinous experience is contingent upon the availability of images in consciousness, not language. The Trinity is such an organizing image. Nicholas of Flue was noted for his silence in the face of his experience, and without the culturally valid image by which to organize the experience he would have been considered mad. The collapse of the image system of Christianity in the Reformation, Jung would argue, resulted in just such cases of madness. Thus there is a sense in which time binds the image in that the image ceases to function satisfactorily as a representation of the numinous at a particular historical point. But precisely the twofold nature of the concept of the boundaries of time leads us, as soon as we recognize the limitation of the image in the provision of meaning, to the following state of affairs. The meaningfulness of time lies in the capacity of images to organize psychic experience transhistorically, and the retreat from reality in schizophrenia is therefore linked to the failure of the image of time. That is to say, for the schizophrenic a retreat from the object means that there is no image of time and hence there is no experience of time.[3] Thus the essential distinction between Brother Klaus and Angelus Silesius is that the Swiss mystic was still able to link his experience to an image from the world outside his psyche. For his German successor this was no longer possible, and there was therefore a necessary inward collapse. But when we transpose this situation to the context of the emergence of psychoanalysis, we confront a serious problem.

Freud's avowed project, we have seen, is to bring the images of the unconscious to language. There they can be tested against reality and dealt with according to the verbal demands of the hermeneutics of suspicion. We have also seen, in Freud's quest for authority, a denial of language, a silence, and the presentation of an image of the primal killing in the form of fainting spells. We may, therefore, suggest that Freud's experience of the unconscious, from which he derived his understanding of incest, ultimately rests on an image and that the image of the primal killing is intended to fill the same requirements for the meaningful organization of the numinous that the Trinity did in Christianity. This suggestion drives a wedge into Freud's system, splitting it in two, the parts of which are psychoanalytic theory and practice on the one hand and, on the other, Freud's biography. But it is Freud's biography, the center of which is his self-analysis, that is the foundation of psychoanalytic theory. The theory calls for the primacy of language over image. But suddenly the foreclosure of language, coupled with an indulgence in images, is necessary to uphold the authority of the theory, thereby pointing to the primacy of the image over language.

In the crisis of authority Freud controls meaning by means of silence and images. This is radically at variance with his theory and, as Jung remarks, the entire process utterly destroys Freud's authority.

Freud's Quest for Timelessness

The Freudian enterprise involves the establishment of a system for the interpretation of human experience. As with many other interpretative systems, it takes as its point of departure a claim to possess a timeless representation of reality. This is critical, for any myth that attempts to define time must itself make a claim to timelessness. However, as with Christianity, these claims can prove problematic or transitory. This is precisely the difficulty with the Freudian enterprise that Jung identified in his objections to the interpretation of incest. The notion of transformation, which Jung tied to a conception of the self-limitation of a myth, implies that Freud's system is not inviolate. The system can be changed into something else, and it contains within itself its own counter-impulse. Indeed, this is why the claim to have access to a timeless realm is so important. Such a claim buttresses the interpretative system against the charge that its first act was an internal definition of time in the constitution of a myth of time. Freud, like others before him, interprets a personal numinous experience and then transposes that interpretation onto the course of history in such a way that its deployment marks the beginning of an age — the age of psychoanalysis.

Collaterally, in the act of positing a dominant myth of time, all other periods of time, all other historical phenomena, must be subsumed under the myth. Thus just as the Old Testament becomes a precursor to Christianity and revolution marks the transition from prehistory to history for Marx, in the case at hand all human endeavor is comprehended by psychoanalysis. Time, in the sense of a meaningful interpretation of history, begins with Freud. Every interpretation that went before was inadequate or an illusion. Time, in other words, finds its boundaries in the myth of psychoanalysis. This means, however, that Freud must isolate the unconscious, as the foundation of all valid understanding, from the vicissitudes of time, for to admit that the unconscious, as Freud's unique realm of insight, is subject to time would deprive him of the ability to make dogmatic claims about the validity of his interpretative insights. Freud's claim to authority requires vindication of the claim that the unconscious does not change its imperatives over time. Freud vindicates this claim by refusing to allow anyone else to return to the primal investigation of the unconscious.

Time and Law

An important question now presents itself: Is the law subject to the vicissitudes of time? We come to this question by way of our discussion of the law in Freud and Hegel in chapter three. There, we recall, I argued that Freud had failed to account for the role of the family in death. Indeed, I asserted that Freud lacks a means of reconciling the individual to death because his project of prohibiting access to the unconscious must take the form of a denial of the family's role in death that is, for Hegel, a means of gaining access to the nether world, the world of the unconscious. We must also recall that Hegel based his vision on a dialectic of the law—divine law and human law—which is not possible for Freud. The point we have now arrived at ties that argument to the problem of time, and we see that in order for Freud to set up his interpretation of the law he must make time stop. This startling conclusion is the result of bringing the argument concerning time into conformity with the primordial moment in Freud's argument: all death is killing.

How is this so? My argument rests on the observation that in the world set up by Freud the only significant death is the death of the primal father, and that death is a killing. Guilt ensues and culture is thereafter bound to the eternal recollection, if not repetition, of that killing. The murder of the primal father gives rise, in turn, to the law—human law in Hegel's terms—and the veneration of the patriarchal totem by the sons absorbs the possibility of divine law in the folds of repression. There is no release from the killing. This brings us to the problem of time by way of the argument developed in this chapter concerning the moment of founding. For if the foundations of culture and the division of the conscious and the unconscious are coterminous with the experience of the primal killing, then there can only be one founding moment, and that is the primordial moment of the killing of the father. The law becomes the cultural expression of that moment and is therefore not subject to time at the level of founding. To repeat, the law in its primordial constitution is tied to the moment of death as killing, and insofar as that moment is primordial and remains forever the death remembered, there can be no subsequent time when the law would be altered.

To argue that founding time stops with the primal killing has a number of consequences. First, we can now interpret the understanding of time proposed by Freud as an argument for the orthodox Freudian interpretation of the Oedipus drama in that to grasp the center of Freudian theory is to grasp the full integration of time and reality in the primordiality of the law. Law and time are joined and, insofar as reality is the balance to instinct, it is an expression of law and time. There is one reality just as there is one time and one law.

But this state of affairs leads us to a deeper issue. The integrity of the law in relation to a new founding time was an essential point of controversy in the Christian era. The Gnostics presented the most radical point of view on this issue: as the counter-argument to orthodox Christian adherence to portions of the old law, their assertion that the emergence of the redeemer destroyed the entire system of authority based on the law was itself grounded in the notion that each individual could come to his or her own experience of founding. The antinomianism of the Gnostics is thus tied to the claim that the presence of new images—in psychoanalytic terms, images from the unconscious—so alters time that nothing persists from a previous age. In Gnosticism, as a consequence, there is a radical disjunction in history that means that the terms of interpretation and the structure of meaning can be fundamentally altered. The fact that in the beginnings of the Christian era there is a system that asserts the primacy of the alteration of the image and of time rather than their continuity— that is, of the ability of the new image to annul previous times and bring forth the new—gives us reason to pursue the relationship between Jung and Freud on the same issue, given the argument concerning Freud's relationship to time and law as well as what we already know of Jung's Gnostic predisposition.

To carry out this analysis, we must address our earlier question of where Freud's psychoanalysis is situated in the emergence of the great systems of meaning. Is it a beginning or is it an end?

Time and Power

What conditions must prevail for a new system of meaning to emerge? How is it that the times are now at the point when other systems of meaning have ceased to inform self-consciousness and Freud's interpretation of the numinous as an expression of the triumph of force, in the form of repression, over meaning, the silence of authority comes to its dominant position? Do timelessness and the retrospective vision of death as killing give shape and meaning to numinous experience at the end of time?

These questions require analysis, and to begin to carry it out I will turn to Nietzsche, whose analysis of the end of meaning dominates the nineteenth century and stands as a precursor of psychoanalysis. Such a comparison has already been suggested by Ricoeur, but I see myself essentially at variance with Ricoeur's notion that Freud shares a common objective with Nietzsche in his quest to expose the hidden, enciphered reality of the psyche (FP 34ff). Rather, I maintain that Freud's subordination of the image to the word, coupled with his closure of the unconscious by way of the image of the primal killing, are attempts to impose the stamp of his own person on a world lacking in meaningful images and caught in language and psychosis. We have seen Freud working out this position in the interpretation of incest, but with the present analysis of time we may discern the mechanism by which Freud sought to achieve this end. Herbert Marcuse also introduced Nietzsche into his discussion of Freud, with particular concern for the question of time and, in his own fashion, he helps to focus the issue. In *Eros and Civilization*, Marcuse writes:

> Will is still a prisoner because it has no power over time: the past not only remains unliberated but, unliberated, continues to mar all liberations. Unless the power of time over life is broken, there can be no freedom: the fact that time does not "recur" sustains the wound of bad conscience: it breeds vengeance and the need for punishment, which in turn perpetuate the past and the sickness to death. (Marcuse, 1966:120)[4]

Marcuse bases his argument on Nietzsche's analysis of the bondage of the will in *Thus Spoke Zarathustra*:

> "To redeem those who lived in the past and to recreate all 'it was' into a 'thus I willed it' — that alone should I call redemption. Will — that is the name of the liberator and joy-bringer; thus I taught you, my friends. But now learn this too: the will itself is a prisoner. Willing liberates; but what is it that puts even the liberator himself in fetters? 'It was' — that is the name of the will's gnashing of teeth and most secret melancholy. Powerless against what has been done, he is an angry spectator of all that is past. The will cannot will backwards; and that he cannot break time and time's covetousness, that is will's loneliest melancholy." (Nietzsche 1978:139)

We now see Freud's interpretation of the unconscious in a larger context. By way of his assertion that the system Ucs is timeless, he establishes as the foundation of our psychic being a place where there is no "it was." "In the unconscious," he writes, "nothing can be brought to an end, nothing is past or forgotten" (SE V:621). This allows him, as the analyst capable of interpreting the expressions of the unconscious, to redeem what the patient thinks is lost in the past. In other words, Freud appears to solve the problem of the will in its bondage to time, thereby achieving emancipation. In this, psychoanalysis appears as a new beginning in time.

The argument of this essay, however, is that Freud's project turns against him; the psychoanalytic hermeneutics of suspicion threatens to undermine the authority of the founder of psychoanalysis. To preserve his authority, Freud must confine that hermeneutics within the domain bounded by his self-disclosure and personal insight. He must bind his followers' understanding of their actions and identities as analysts within the timeless frame of his own self-understanding.

As we have seen, Freud accomplishes this confinement, and vindicates his authority, by proposing an interpretation of the psyche based on the primacy of repression and the retrospective vision of death as killing. It is in terms of this interpretation that Freud can indeed be said to offer redemption, but only at the price of one's acknowledgment that things can never change for the psyche. In the retrospective temporal orientation of Freud's system, the timelessness of the unconscious is indissolubly tied to repression and death, and the limited release the system offers is bought at the price of even greater domination: to accept Freud's offer of a way out is to admit that one exists in a world without a future, for in a world in which the death of the primal patriarch is the center of culture, there is no possibility for the emergence of new meanings in a time that is not governed by that death. There is no future that is anything beyond the increasingly complex and burdensome repetition of the past.

The internal demands of Freud's argument turn the project of emancipation inside out. As his personal experience discloses the timelessness of the unconscious, as his life story becomes our collective myth, Freud's biography becomes the metabiography determining all experiences and lives. But to move from time to timelessness, life to myth, biography to metabiography is to leave behind the world of change and development; for Freud to declare the fundamental structures and functions of the psyche to be outside time is, in effect, to immortalize his own psyche, his own being. Every child that comes into the world must pass through the phases of life which Freud has revealed, and only Freud can offer an explanation of why this is so. With this, Freud's closure of the unconscious, by way of his interpretation of the primal myth of incest and the analytics of the primacy of repression, brings the possibility of finding new meaning to an end. Thus we answer our question concerning Freud's place in the constitution of an age; his system, taken on its own terms, marks the end of meaning.

Freud's system nevertheless stands as a major force in our cultural discourse. That this should be the case when we have just argued that the system marks the end of meaning raises again the question of why Freud should exercise such epochal influence. It is also the case that only by giving an account of why Freud is possible at this time can we recover the possibility of meaning. Why this is so will become clear in the next chapter. There we will explore Jung's understanding of the relationship of time and psyche, which he works out in his interpretation of the phenomenon of projection, as the alternative by which a recovery of meaning may be accomplished by way of an epochal vision that encompasses the possibility of a system such as Freud's coming to occupy the place it does. But this displacement of Freud's project into Jung's system of interpretation can only take place if we can locate the two projects in a topography that is common to both. To a substantial degree, we now see, the argument of this essay has sought to define that place, and it presents itself now in the form of the topography mapped by the conflict between the two interpretations given to the temporal horizon of the unconscious: is the temporal horizon futural or retrospective?

This distinction, on which the struggle rests, and from which we will finally be able to draw the answer to our question of Freud's place in our culture, is prefigured by Nietzsche when he writes that the question of creativity in romanticism resolves itself into the question of whether the primacy of "the desire to fix, to immortalize, the desire for *being* promoted creation, or the desire for destruction, for change, for *becoming*" (Nietzsche 1974:329). That Jung falls within the ambit of European romanticism is not a remarkable claim, but it is only in the context of the analysis of Freud's relationship to time and to Jung that we clearly see that Freud is also an expression of the romantic impulse. In his attempt to establish the primacy of his own experience for all subsequent acts of self-understanding, he falls into a particular form of romanticism which Nietzsche defines as an expression of the person of tyrannical will who

> suffers deeply, who struggles, is tormented, and would like to turn what is most personal, singular, and narrow, the real idiosyncrasy of his suffering, into binding law and compulsion — one who, as it were, revenges himself on all things by forcing his own image, the image of his torture, on them, branding them with it. This last version is romantic pessimism in its most expressive form, whether it be Schopenhauer's philosophy of will or Wagner's music — romantic pessimism, the last great event in the fate of our culture. (Nietzsche 1974:330)

Here we find the key to our twofold questioning of Freud. Insofar as Freud's vision of the unconscious is retrospective and confines meaning within the boundary of the killing of the primal father, meaning ends in the repetition of the past. And insofar as the retrospective project is an expression of the will to immortalize his own suffering, Freud becomes part of a tyranny of the end itself that has the form of romantic pessimism. We may penetrate the apparent circularity of this argument by recalling the notion of the boundaries of time with which we began this chapter. There we saw that myth can give time its meaning but also that time, in the form of a life cycle of the myth, can bind meaning. What we confront in Freud is the expression of the quest for meaning in a world where the end of meaning has become possible. Freud's myth, in other words, is the myth of the end of meaning. Freud emerges in a world where the possibility of his myth is in the position of primacy. Only a myth of the end of meaning can define time at the point when time has exhausted a myth of meaning.

Seven

Projection and the Life of Phantasy

I. Projection

Jung's View of Time and the Unconscious

Jung, too, embraced the notion that the unconscious was essentially timeless. His interpretation, however, offers a prospective vision of meaning that promises to show the way out of the problematic of authority in Freud. Thus, in 1913, Jung was intent on rejecting the notion of infantile sexuality on the grounds that things did change for the psyche. At that time he wrote that "it makes no difference that there were already conflicts in childhood, for the conflicts of childhood are different from the conflicts of adults" (CW 4:354). This conception of the role of conflict becomes decisive for Jung's therapeutic technique when, for example, he maintains that the first question to be asked in the interpretation of a dream is what conflict the person is facing at the time when the dream takes place (CW16:330). At least in part, Jung based his conclusion about the timeliness of the activity of the psyche on the analysis conducted in *Transformations*, which concluded that the Oedipus complex could be seen in many different lights through the course of an individual's life. Only on certain occasions could the complex be said to have the particular sexual and familial significance attributed to it by Freud. The true message of the myth, and the issue faced in dealing with the complex was not overcoming incestuous impulses, but rather the development of the individual through a series of stages. At each stage the motif of sacrifice, particularly the sacrifices surrounding the figure of the mother, dominates the myth and orients us towards the role of the unconscious in establishing the sense of time.

The significance of Jung's alternative vision becomes clear if we return to Freud's interpretation of the timelessness of unconscious representations and his view of the possibility of a psychoanalysis of history. Not only is the conflict of the adult the same as the conflict of the child, the conflicts of history are the same conflicts as those uncovered by Freud in his self-analysis. At the philosophical level this assertion constitutes a principle of biographical intelligibility, or metabiography, in that the structure of the unconscious, as he sees it, allows Freud to assert the transparency of history, both personal and cultural. In other words, as psychoanalysts we may return to the worlds of Leonardo or of Moses and confidently work out the psychological issues that preoccupied them.

Jung, on the other hand, maintained that while sexuality may very well be the fundamental conflict of the late nineteenth century, in which case Freud should be thanked for addressing it as he did, there is no reason to assume that it is the conflict appropriate to the analysis of other cultures or of the ancient traditions antedating Western culture. This objection on Jung's part puts us in the position of seeing just how emphatically Freud is attempting to carry out the project of romantic pessimism, as described by Nietzsche, in that he seeks, in his conception of the unconscious, to impose the nature of his own being on becoming *everything has always been as it now is in me.*

The reason that such an imposition is possible is that the analytic armamentation of the Freudian psychoanalyst, the hermeneutics of suspicion, which takes objections to the theory as confirmation of its truth, turns against any attempt to challenge the assertion of the timelessness of the representations of the unconscious. Thus there is no doctrine of emancipation in Freud once he deploys his system of analysis under the banner of repression, as we have already seen. But if the deployment of the analytic enterprise proceeds differently, we begin to see the way out.

The Primacy of Projection

The alternative, which yields an epochal view of the psyche rather than the constant view which Freud proposed, derives from the primacy of projection. Indeed, Jung would claim that the resistance of the patient, which Freud takes to be proof positive of repression at work, is the result of projection. Here I will draw on a remark Jung made in 1931 because of its particular clarity on this point. It is interesting to note, as well, the central position given to the first dream in a series:

> Initial dreams are often amazingly lucid and clear-cut. But as the work of analysis progresses, the dreams tend to lose their clarity. If, by way of exception, they keep it we can be sure that the analysis has not yet touched on some important layer of the personality. As a rule, dreams get more and more opaque and blurred soon after the beginning of the treatment, and this makes the interpretation increasingly difficult. A further difficulty is that a point may soon be reached where, if the truth be told, the doctor no longer understands the situation as a whole. That he does not understand is proved by the fact that the dreams become increasingly obscure, for we all know that their "obscurity" is a purely subjective opinion of the doctor. To the understanding nothing is obscure; it is only when we do not understand that things appear unintelligible and muddled. In themselves dreams are naturally clear; that is, they are just what they must be under the given circumstances. If, from a later stage of treatment or from a distance of some years, we look back at these unintelligible dreams, we are often astounded at our own blindness. Thus when, as the analysis proceeds, we come upon dreams that are strikingly obscure in comparison with the illuminating initial dreams, the doctor should not be too ready to accuse the dreams of confusion or the patient of deliberate resistance; he would do better to take these findings as a sign of his own growing inability to understand just as the psychiatrist who calls his patient "confused" should recognize that this is a projection and should rather call himself confused, because in reality it is he whose wits are confused by the patient's peculiar behavior. Moreover it is therapeutically very important for the doctor to admit his lack of understanding in time, for nothing is more unbearable to the patient than to be always understood. (CW 16:313)

This passage alerts us to the significance Jung places on interpreting the analyst's countertransference. A less Freudian point of view would be hard to find. What is important to note is that "to be always understood" is taken by Jung to be the most unbearable aspect of psychoanalysis. What Jung is arguing is that it is precisely the intelligibility principle in Freud that is the greatest threat to the patient. The project of the post-Freudian, for whom Jung is the model, is therefore to escape from the transparent world of Freud and from the assertion of power premised on Freud's particular interpretation of the timelessness of the unconscious. But as I have already argued in detail, Freud prohibits access to the unconscious, and, having introduced the problem of temporality in chapter six, we are in the position of developing an argument that to gain access to the unconscious and offer a counter-interpretation to Freud's, implicates one in proposing an alternative vision of the relationship of time and psyche. Jung accomplishes this by way of a fundamental alteration of the concept of projection.

Freud's Interpretation of Projection

The concept of projection was introduced into psychoanalysis by Freud, who appropriated the term from the neurologist Meynert, one of his teachers. Originally, the concept dealt with the representation of the body in the cerebral cortex. How, for example, does an olfactory sensation come to be sensed in the nose when the neurological location of the sensation is in reality isolated within the cortex? Meynert proposed that the cortex "projects" its impression back into its physiological source (Meynert 1885:79 ff). A certain reciprocity is at work, however, in that a smell is in fact in the nose before it is in the cortex and so, Meynert went on, the nose is, in a sense, "projected" onto the cortex by the nervous system.

Freud altered the meaning of projection dramatically, not the least by removing the sense of reciprocity. His conception viewed projection as a defense mechanism associated, as we have already seen, with the experience of being able to interact with one's physical environment. Threatening mental activities are projected into the world of physical objects with the purpose of manipulating them by manipulating the objects. This frequently takes the form of projecting what one most fears in oneself onto the other, where an attempt can be made to manipulate the problem. A more radical form of projection occurs in paranoia where an entire system of fear is projected onto the outside world.

Although Freud investigated projection in relation to paranoia in the Schreber case of 1911, he did not limit use of the term to disturbed or abnormal consciousness. Projection and paranoia are thus not synonymous. Rather, projection is an essential constituent of the comprehension of the world, especially of the mythological or religious conception of events. In 1901 Freud took up this theme in *The Psychopathology of Everyday Life* in a manner that brings into focus the far reaching significance of projection:

> In point of time, I believe that a large part of the mythological view of the world, which extends a long way into the most modern religions, is nothing but psychology projected into the external world. The obscure recognition (the endopsychic perception, as it were) of psychical factors and relations in the unconscious is mirrored. . . in the constitution of a supernatural reality, which is destined to be changed back once more by science into the psychology of the unconscious. (SE VI:258f)

Animism

Freud continues to develop the notion that psychology will return us "once more" to the originative psychology of the unconscious in *Totem and Taboo*. There he asserts the primacy of psychology in the origins of the most elementary religious phenomenon, animism:

> Animism is a system of thought. It does not merely give an explanation of a particular phenomenon but allows us to grasp the whole universe as a single unity from a single point of view. The human race, if we are to follow the authorities, have in the course of ages developed three such systems of thought three great pictures of the universe: animistic (or mythological), religious and scientific. Of these, animism, the first to be created, is perhaps the one which is most consistent and exhaustive and which gives a truly complete explanation of the nature of the universe. The first human *Weltanschauung* is a psychological theory. (SE XIII:77)

The outline Freud presents in this passage points to the fact that animism is not itself a religion but is rather the foundation for the possibility of religion (SE XIII:77). Going a step further, following the anthropologists Hubert and Mauss, Freud identifies magic as animism's effective technique (SE XIII:78). Freud then turns to Frazer's discussion of magic, which focuses on the psychic component. He quotes Frazer to the effect that "men mistook the order of their ideas for the order of nature, and hence imagined that the control which they have, or seem to have, over their thoughts, permitted them to exercise a corresponding control over things" (SE XIII:83). From this conception of magic Freud concludes that "the principle governing magic, the technique of the animistic mode of thinking, is the principle of the 'omnipotence of thought' " (SE XIII:85). In the modern world, the omnipotence of thought is associated with obsessional neurosis. In the animistic world, however, the omnipotence of thought was the very foundation for understanding, a fact that recalls us to our discussion of killing, death, and Freud's desire to die (chapter four).

Death and Projection

The discussion of projection and the emergence of mythologies in *Totem and Taboo* is intimately bound up with the analysis of primal killing discussed previously. In the second essay of *Totem*, which precedes the discussion of animism, Freud claims that the confrontation with death provokes projection as a defense against negative feelings harbored against the dead while they were still alive (SE XIII:61). In the projection, the negative feelings are instantiated in the spirit of the dead person that must be avoided, propitiated, or otherwise dealt with in a manner that will allow the negative feelings to be discharged. Thus the result of the projection is the constitution of a spirit world that is not under the control of the thoughts of the person. This moment of constitution represents a breakdown of the experience of the omnipotence of thought and a dissociation of psychic activity under the impact of projection.

The constitution of a realm of spirits by primitive cultures requires, on Freud's reading, a form of renunciation. The renunciation is manifested as projection, which is an attempt to gain relief from the conflicts of psychic activity the negative feelings toward the dead person. Contrary to what other commentators claim, Freud contends that it is not the intellectual problem of death but its attendant emotional conflicts that require resolution (SE XIII:92f). Since all thoughts about a certain situation cannot be expressed, one or another must be projected. Freud looks on this crisis as the prototype of the psychological understanding of the unconscious:

> When we, no less than primitive man, project something into external reality, what is happening must surely be this: we are recognizing the existence of two states one in which something is directly given to the senses and to consciousness (that is, is present to them), and

alongside it another, in which the same thing is latent but capable of re-appearing. In short, we are recognizing the co-existence of perception and memory, or, putting it more generally, the existence of unconscious mental processes alongside the conscious ones. (SE XIII:93f)

This passage embeds projection in the larger Freudian system. The phenomenology of projection rests, for Freud, on the already established disjunction between conscious and unconscious. It rests, in other words, on repression, and particularly on primal repression. Indeed, the entire discussion of the origins of animism in projection, that is, the origin of religious systems out of the conflict engendered by death, takes the primal killings as its point of departure. Following the act of primal killing, the dead father becomes the object of fear and veneration in the totem feast. But this can only occur if the unconscious has already been established by way of primal repression, which itself focuses on the desire to kill the father. Thus projection is a product of repression and reflects a wish to manipulate repressed contents of the unconscious as one manipulates reality.

Jung: Primal Projection

During the first years of their association, Jung was basically in agreement with Freud on the role of the unconscious in the analysis of projection. This continued in the writing of *Transformations* (CW 5:93). The issues that finally divided them nevertheless concerned the understanding of the relationship between projection and the unconscious.

Prior to 1912 Jung had begun to elaborate a theory of projection beyond what Freud had developed. The crucial, early passage, which sets up Jung's entire future vision of the psyche under the rubric of the primacy of projection, appears in a footnote to the original version of *Transformations*:[1]

> The projection into the "cosmic" is the primitive privilege of the libido, for it enters into our perception naturally through all the avenues of the senses, apparently from without, and in the form of pain and pleasure connected with the objects. This we attribute to the object without further thought, and we are inclined, in spite of our philosophic considerations, to seek the causes in the object, which

often has very little concern with it. Here . . . belong all the miraculous stories of cosmic events, phenomena occurring at the birth and death of heroes. (The Star of Bethlehem; earthquakes, the rending asunder of the temple hangings, etc., at the death of Christ.) The omnipotence of God is the manifest omnipotence of the libido, the only actual doer of wonders which we know. The symptom described by Freud, as the "omnipotence of thought" in Compulsion Neuroses arises from the "sexualizing" of the intellect. The historical parallel for this is the magical omnipotence of the mystic, attained by introversion. The "omnipotence of thought" corresponds to the identification with God of the paranoiac, arrived at similarly through introversion. (Jung 1916:505f)

Here we see not only the primacy of projection but also what may be termed "primal projection" insofar as recognition of the world itself rests on a primordial investiture of the world with psychic energy, libido.

In 1920, in an appendix to his major work *Psychological Types*, Jung continued to place projection in this central role. There he defined projection in contrast to introjection, which is the assimilation of subject to object. Projection is an act of dissimulation, and as such it is an act of alienation from the object and the contents projected onto it:

Projection results from the archaic identity of subject and object, but is properly so called only when the need to dissolve the identity with the object becomes a disturbing factor, i.e., when the absence of the projected content is a hindrance to adaptation and its withdrawal into the subject has become desirable. From this moment the previous partial identity acquires the character of a projection. The term projection therefore signifies a state of identity that has become noticeable, an object of criticism, whether it be the self-criticism of the subject or the objective criticism of another. (CW 6:783)

What Jung suggests in this passage is that our fundamental experience of the world is based on projection, which only becomes noticeable when we withdraw from the object on which the projection rests. Applied to Freud's analysis of the primal horde, Jung would seem to say that only this investment of libido by way of primal projection allows the son to recognize the primal father in the first place. Without this primordial recognition, primal repression cannot take place. Recognition of emotional investment in the object must have precedence or else we would have nothing but random violence. This would be totally out of keeping with Freud's model and would vindicate Jung's argument that at the most primordial level there is no father. It is the case, of course, that in the myth itself, Oedipus does not recognize his father at the crossroads. Laius is simply an indifferent violent male. To make Freud's interpretation of Oedipus primordial, the argument must be that the son recognizes the father, as opposed to an indifferent male presence, through primal projection. This means, however, that the son recognizes himself in the father, a claim with far-reaching implications for the interpretation of incest.

Projection: Oedipus Reinterpreted

To grasp the significance of Jung's argument we must turn back to the discussion of incest and attempt an interpretation based on the notion of primal projection. A primordial identity between father and son would be the result of primal projection. With the passage of time this identity would necessarily break down as the son sought to claim an independent place in the world and importantly as the father prepared to leave the world in death, the symbolization of this recognition being the "accidental" but fated encounter of Laius and Oedipus at the crossroads. To continue the primordial identity would bind both father and son in their quest for individual identity. The movement to independence makes projection noticeable in the form of a threat to the father and restraint on the son. Were they truly to break away from one another, nothing should be left of the primal projection. But those aspects of primordial identity that hold fast to the person of the father threaten to tear gaps in the emergent personality of the son. The converse is also the case, and the proposal can be made that it is precisely the primordial identity with the strength of the father that, in Freud's myth of the primal killing, gives the son the power to act to kill the father. However, insofar as primal projections have not been totally withdrawn, to kill the father is to kill that part of oneself that remains with the father as projection. With this formulation we come to a new and startling interpretation of the meaning of totemic veneration: it is an attempt to mitigate an unconscious sense of one's own suicide or self-murder. Phrased differently, veneration allows a continuation of the projected linkage in a form that allows one to preserve one's self-identity in the face of the death of the revered other who carries our projections.

Reading Jung's interpretation of projection in this manner also deepens our understanding of the place of the mother in the incest drama. Since the primordial identity between father and son is an unconscious identity, its breakdown in the withdrawal of projection brings with it a profound activation of the unconscious — symbolized in *Oedipus* by the oracle at Delphi, the Sphinx, Jocasta, and the Earth — at each successive step in individuation. A profound dialectical movement is set in motion by this activation. Continuing to take Oedipus as our example, we can now see that the overcoming of the father is precipitated by an oracular encounter with the Great Mother — the unconscious in our interpretation of psychoanalysis — and is followed by the destruction of an effigy of the unconscious, the assumption of the place of the father by the son, and an encounter with a deeper representative of the father by way of the action of the unconscious. Thus the predictions of the oracle at Delphi, who speaks out of the earth, lead to the killing of Laius and the suicide of the Sphinx. Again, Delphi initiates Oedipus's confrontation with Tiresias and the suicide of Jocasta, accompanied, of course, by Oedipus's self-blinding, which brings him into a strange conformity with his former soul-guide, Tiresias, who is blind but nevertheless sees clearly, just as the death of the Sphinx allowed him to occupy the position of his father, Laius. In its turn the blinding conforms Oedipus to the final effigy of the Great Mother, Antigone, who leads him on his final quest for a resting place. Only in the end is Oedipus able to pass a blessing to his own successor, Theseus, as he returns to the Earth from whom all the calls to individuation originally emerged.

The entire drama becomes, by way of this interpretation, a pilgrim's progress of the soul seeking individual completeness. But it only takes on this character when viewed from the point of view of primal projection, and successive and ever deeper encounters with the unconscious. Primal repression and succeeding acts of repression proper, which are intended to prohibit access to the unconscious, cannot account for the pattern of personal growth that is evident in the myth. Indeed, the positing of the primacy of repression entails rejection of growth by attributing the images of growth to the process of censorship. We can see, therefore, that the system chosen to constitute the psychic distinction between conscious and unconscious is decisive for the subsequent interpretation of psychodynamic data.

Jung's struggle with Freud also comes under this interpretation; we can now see Jung's progress away from Freud as a performance of the reinterpreted Oedipus drama. Jung, the child, is called away from his father by the dreams of the unconscious, where it is the voice of the mother that speaks to him. He destroys an effigy of the unconscious as he solves the riddle of Helene's seances and assumes the place of his father as a healer of souls. He then moves to a deeper encounter with the unconscious in the association with Freud. His struggle with Freud, like that of Oedipus with Tiresias, is characterized by prohibition and an even deeper descent into the unconscious by way of a form of self-blinding in Jung's loss of the Freudian paradigm, which is itself an effigy of the unconscious. It is also likely that Jung's peculiar relationships with his wife, Emma, and his mistress, Toni Wolff, provide further clues to the course of this development. It appears that Wolff's recovery from a schizophrenic state enabled Jung to cope with his own encounter with the unconscious. This final descent took the form, in Jung's own estimation, of a psychoticlike state. It is to this encounter that we must now turn.

II. The Life of Phantasy

Jung's Encounter with the Unconscious

In his autobiography Jung devotes an entire chapter to the confrontation with the unconscious that followed his break with Freud. During this period, he was beset by dreams of death and widespread destruction, which he later associated with the political events of the time, particularly the First World War. At the same time, however, the motif of death and the presence of "the dead" prompted Jung to hypothesize that archaic elements in the psyche spontaneously returned to consciousness in response to the demands of the moment. This notion, which builds on the earlier theory of the teleology of the psyche and which foreshadowed the emergence of his theory of archetypes, came to him as much through dreams and phantasies as through conscious investigations (MDR 173). Similarly, during this period Jung engaged in forms of childlike play, building a village out of stones found on the lake shore (MDR 174).

Throughout his account of this period, phantasy is depicted as equal if not superior to dreaming. Jung's project was to allow the unconscious to come forward in his life and reveal itself to him. I take it that this is not unlike Freud's project of self-analysis. For Jung the opening up of the unconscious led to an increasing sense of crisis. The very clear impression one gets from the account is that Jung was dangerously close to an outright breakdown during this period:

> An incessant stream of fantasies had been released, and I did my best not to lose my head but to find some way to understand these strange things. I stood helpless before an alien world; everything in it seemed difficult and incomprehensible. I was living in a constant state of tension; often I felt as if gigantic blocks of stone were tumbling down upon me. One thunderstorm followed another. My enduring these storms was a question of brute strength. Others have been shattered by them Nietzsche, and Holderlin, and many others. But there was a daemonic strength in me, and from the beginning there was no doubt in my mind that I must find the meaning of what I was experiencing in these fantasies. (MDR 176f)

As the phantasy world continued to elaborate itself, the primacy of the image became increasingly important for Jung. "To the extent that I managed to translate the emotions into images," he writes, "that is to say, to find the images which were concealed in the emotions I was inwardly calmed and reassured" (MDR 177). Indeed, not to locate the images that would embody the emotions that threatened to overwhelm him would have resulted, Jung writes, in his being "torn to pieces by them" (MDR 177). This process continued until Jung began to encounter a series of distinct personal figures emerging from the unconscious. These figures were eventually recognized as embodiments of the archetypes, representations of essentially autonomous and numinous psychic phenomena.[2] Among the figures encountered by Jung during this period was a wise old man, to whom he gave the name Philemon. With the emergence of the image of Philemon in the phantasy world of Jung's encounter with the unconscious we may again pick up the thread of Gnosticism that informs Jung's personal myth system. According to Jung, "Philemon was a pagan and brought with him an Egypto-Hellenistic atmosphere with a Gnostic coloration" (MDR 182). Philemon became the teacher in Jung's phantasy, thereby replacing Freud, and revealed the mysteries of the psyche to him. The period of unconscious stimulation and phantasy production continued in this manner until 1916 when, Jung records, he began to change (MDR 189). This marks Jung's emergence from his radical encounter with the unconscious. The signpost of the change in Jung's works draws us dramatically into his Gnostic myth:

> In 1916 I felt an urge to give shape to something. I was compelled from within, as it were, to formulate and express what might have been said by Philemon. This was how the *Septem Sermones ad Mortuos* with its peculiar language came into being. (MDR 190)

The Sermons

Septem Sermones ad Mortuos was composed during a three-day crisis when the "spirits of the dead" came to Jung's home demanding recognition. This strange occurrence appears to have been a collective event, witnessed, in some sense, by other members of Jung's household. A pervasive sense of the house being crowded with people, bells ringing when no one was at the door, and similar phenomena marked the experience (MDR 190ff). At this point the *Sermons* themselves take up the narrative:

> The dead came back from Jerusalem, where they found not what they sought. They prayed me let them in and besought my word, and thus I began my teaching. (MDR 378)

The debt to Nietzsche is painful and, indeed, in their English version the *Sermons* are rendered in a mannered biblical style reminiscent of early translations of *Thus Spoke Zarathustra*. Just as Nietzsche assumed the persona of Zarathustra to produce his monumental work, so Jung assumes a persona, that of the second-century Gnostic Basilides, to preach his sermons to the dead.[3]

In the *Sermons* the spirits of the dead seek release from this world, demanding answers to questions about gods and devils, the Gnostic deity Abraxas, and sexuality. Sermons one through six fail to satisfy the dead, for they continue to return with more questions and usually raise a protest against the teaching they receive. Finally, in the seventh sermon, almost as an afterthought, the dead ask to be taught about man. This request shapes a certain symmetry in the sermons since at the end of Sermo VII, "the dead were silent and ascended like the smoke above the herdsman's fire, who through the night kept watch over his flock" (MDR 389f). This scene allows us to conclude that what had not been found in Jerusalem is found in this sermon. Jung-Basilides writes:

> Man is a gateway, through which from the outer pass into the inner world; out of the greater into the smaller world. Small and transitory is man. Already he is behind you, and once again ye find yourselves in endless space, in the smaller and innermost infinity. At immeasurable distance standeth one single star in the zenith.
> This is the one god of this one man. This is his world, his pleroma, his divinity.
> In this world is man Abraxas, the creator and the destroyer of his own world. (MDR 389)

Jung's theme is one of man as a point of transition in some religio-metaphysical space. In other words, the being "man" is singularly transitory. There is in the seventh sermon, in addition, a sense of the individualization of religion. Each person is able to constitute an appropriate god-image. This highlights the curious transition between outer and inner worlds that brings with it the assumption by man himself of the role of Abraxas, the unknown god of the Gnostics, already introduced by Jung-Basilides in Sermo II.

The power of Abraxas consists in the ability to found a world. The source of the inward turn, however, is not immediately clear. While we can conceive of the constitution of the god within, we must look deeper still to find the original source. This point of origin is prefigured throughout the sermons in the mythic motif of the return of the dead; clearly, given Jung's psychic state, a metaphor for the explosion of the contents of the unconscious. The problem that the teaching ultimately seeks to resolve, and which ultimately concerns the dead, is precisely the problem of death and the unconscious. This claim is upheld by Jung:

> This Star is the god and goal of man.
> This Star is the one guiding god. In him goeth man to his rest.
> Toward him goeth the long journey of the soul after death. In him

shineth forth as light all that man bringeth back from the greater world. To this one god man shall pray.

Prayer increaseth the light of the Star. It casteth a bridge over death. It prepareth life for the smaller world and assuageth the hopeless desires of the greater.

When the greater world waxeth cold, burneth the Star. (MDR 389)

The goal of the dead who have come to learn from him is thus constituted in the interior world. The problem, of course, is that the goal of this inner world is as much a creation as is the god of the now lost outer world. He is established, as was the macrocosmic god, by the power of Abraxas. But the place of Abraxas, on the occasion of the inward turn, is assumed by man. The goal is, therefore, constituted by those who seek the goal. This circumstance requires a remarkable double movement on the part of man if he is to keep his god of the inner world:

Between man and his god there standeth nothing, so long as man can turn away his eyes from the flaming spectacle of Abraxas. (MDR 389)

But to do this man must first constitute his world and then forget his act of constitution and live within the world. Man must create the god he will worship and then turn away from his very act of creation.

How are we to make sense of this? As I will show in a moment, Jung's major work of this period, *Psychological Types*, contributes to our understanding of world constitution as a problem of psychoanalytic theory. But the *Sermons*, and the lived experiences that preceded and surrounded their composition, provide us with indispensable existential data for understanding Jung. After the break with Freud, Jung embarked on his own exploration of the unconscious. This was, as I have argued, precisely what Freud sought to prevent. During this encounter Jung's personal Gnostic mythology emerged, at long last, in explicit form. This could only happen when phantasy gained access to consciousness. And the message of the phantasy, finally articulated in the seventh sermon to the dead, was that each person could create his or her own world, his or her own mythology, thereby releasing the dead to float off like the smoke of a camp fire.

131

With this in mind we may turn to a more theoretical consideration of phantasy, which will bring us back to the discussion of primal repression and primal projection.

Phantasy

What, then, is the nature of this engine of the psyche that eventually comes to dominate Jung's theories? In *Types*, Jung writes:

> Fantasy . . . seems to me the clearest expression of the specific activity of the psyche. It is, pre-eminently, the creative activity from which the answers to all answerable questions come; it is the mother of all possibilities, where, like all psychological opposites, the inner and outer worlds are joined together in living union. Fantasy it was and ever is which fashions the bridge between the irreconcilable claims of subject and object, introversion and extraversion. In fantasy alone both mechanisms are united. (CW 6:78)

And in the unity established by phantasy the psyche finds the means to "create reality every day" (CW 6:78). Phantasy provides the glue holding reality and the psyche together, for "there is no psychic function that, through fantasy, is not inextricably bound up with the other psychic functions" (CW6:78).

In developing his conception of phantasy, Jung is particularly interested in the phenomena of religion and poetry. In other words, we are still in the area of concern to which Freud turned in *Totem and Taboo* and Jung in *Transformations*, and which precipitated much of the controversy between the two men. This is not accidental. There is an organic link, which exists in both Freud and Jung, between the primacy of either repression or projection, phantasy, and the emergence of major cultural forces such as the great religions. Since it is my contention that Freud's objective in the deployment of psychoanalytic theory is to set up a myth that will dominate an age, Jung's analysis of phantasy must account for the possibility and the nature of such a constituting act on Freud's part and for Jung's own resistance to it. Paradoxically, this leads to the realization that psychoanalysis is, in its essence, a phantasy.

Phantasy and Culture

Let me illustrate how psychoanalysis can be seen as a phantasy by returning to our paradigm of the constitution of a cultural force, the emergence of the Christian era and its attendant activity over the centuries. Jung sees the emergence of the Christian worldview as the triumph and absolutization of the phantasy of a small group. To succeed the Christian had to suppress or absorb all other systems of phantasy expressing the experience of the unconscious in other individuals. Christianity achieves this end by recourse to a dogmatic system of symbols. This impulse to overcome the phantasy of the other, however, requires that the phantasy products of one particular individual, the founder of the religion, be given absolute status:

> Whenever we observe a religion being born, we see how the doctrinal figures flow into the founder himself as revelations, in other words as concretizations of his unconscious fantasy. The forms welling up from his unconscious are declared to be universally valid and thus replace the individual fantasies of others. (CW 6:80)

Furthermore, the founder is responsible for the interpretation of his phantasies, and it is the appropriateness of the interpretation that establishes beyond a doubt the nature of the religion. In the case of Jesus, Jung contends, an example of this act of primal self-interpretation is found in the temptations in the wilderness where the possibility of an interpretation based on a worldly kingdom is presented within the phantasy system itself, only to be rejected by Jesus in favor of an interpretation based on a heavenly conception of kingship that allows the religious aspect of the phantasy to gain dominance (CW6:80). Once the symbols from the unconscious are absolutized and appropriately interpreted, the postulation of any other phantasy system becomes an expression of heresy. This brings us back to the Gnostics (CW 6:81f).

Jung is not contending that the phantasy system of the founder of a religion should be confused with the simple ravings of the insane, and he takes the example of Jesus's response to the temptation in the wilderness as a measure of the subtlety and psychic order in religious phantasy. Indeed, what is at stake in the founding of a religion is a genuine response to the *Zeitgeist*:

> The relationship of the individual to his fantasy is very largely con-
> ditioned by his relationship to the unconscious in general, and this in
> turn is conditioned in particular by the spirit of the age. (CW 6.80)

In the case of Christianity this meant a response to the collapse, in classical antiquity, of the efficacy of classical symbolization and rite. Jung goes on to argue that the religious impulse of late antiquity was best exemplified by such individuals as Origen and Tertullian, who reacted to the new demands of the Christian religion by an amputation or sacrifice of some aspect of their being that had been venerated in the older systems. In the case of Origen this meant literal self-castration, and in the case of Tertullian a total rejection of the rational intellect where matters of religion were concerned, an intellectual castration as it were. Here we return to Jung's argument in *Transformations*, where sacrifice was the means by which the hero moved beyond the mother, beyond the encounter with the unconscious (as was the self-blinding of Oedipus). This reflects a turning inward, or recovery, of the psychic energy previously projected into the world and signified by the sacrificed element. Turned inward, the flow of energy activates the symbol-forming capacity of the unconscious, and the symbols thus generated become a new spiritual reality of intense psychic importance that replaces the amputated or sacrificed capacity. The symbol can become concrete by becoming a new but no longer identifiable projection that finds its object in the figure of the founder of the religion. Thus the old projection, say into the veneration of the intellect in Greek philosophy, becomes known as a projection, an act of idolatry the Christian would say, when the age is about to change its symbols. The energy released by the withdrawal of the projection the rejection of idolatry allows the formation of new symbols that are projected in what I have characterized as a primal projection, onto the figure of the founder. This process is identical to that suggested in the interpretation of the Oedipus myth developed above.

At this point the reader might well object that primal projection has become confused with secondary projections because "primal" implies an initial act of constitution. Thus primal repression in Freud is tied to the primal killing that is ahistorical, whereas the present argument points to a primal projection located in history. This, however, is precisely the point at which the argument concerning the boundaries of time returns to our interpretation of psychoanalysis. Primal projection occurs "in history" as in the case of Christianity, in the following manner. In the projection that accompanies the Christian era one clearly finds all the representations of a "world founding" that one would associate with a "cosmic" event. In particular, time is altered in the emergence of the symbolism of the Christian era, and a "new time" may now be seen as the proof mark of a primal projection.

This is, schematically, the mechanism by which the notion I term the life cycle of the myth comes into being, and it points to the strongly dialectical sense of the growth of religion where the initial deployment of a set of symbols by the founder provokes symbol formation in his followers by calling into question previously deployed mythologies. In other words, a complete theology is constituted by the progressive elaboration of a set of primal symbols. Brother Klaus contributes, in this way, to the life of the Christian myth. But he depends on the continued presence and viability of the primal symbols that have a life-span that has run out, in the Christian case, by the time Angelus Silesius comes on the scene.

Jung's Dialectic of the Spirit

Jung is sensitive to the many currents flowing in the times that saw the emergence of Christianity. In keeping with the theme of *Psychological Types* he is intent to show how these currents reflected the distinction between introversion and extraversion, between interest in the interior world and interest in the external world. In the case of Christianity the notion of love as an essential aspect of religious commitment is based on an essentially extraverted orientation directed toward the object (CW 6:191). This religious interest in the object and particularly the objective individual results in the overcoming of classical social elitism. Just as there is, in Jung, a strongly dialectical sense of the constitution of religion proper, a dialectic can now be set up on the social level that closely resembles Hegel's analysis of the role of Christianity in world history. Jung writes:

> Just as the ancients, with an eye to individual development, catered to the well-being of an upper class by an almost total suppression of the great majority of the common people (helots, slaves), the Christian

135

world reached a condition of collective culture by transferring this same process, as far as possible, to the psychological sphere *within* the individual himself—raising it, one might say, to the subjective level. As the chief value of the individual was proclaimed by Christian dogma to be an imperishable soul, it was no longer possible for the inferior majority of the people to be suppressed in actual fact for the freedom of a more valuable minority. Instead, the more valuable function within the individual was preferred above the inferior functions. In this way the chief importance was attached to the one valued function, to the detriment of all the rest. Psychologically this meant that the external form of society in classical civilization was transferred into the subject. . . . By means of this psychological process a collective culture gradually came into existence, in which the "rights of men" were guaranteed for the individual to an immeasurably greater degree than in antiquity. But it had the disadvantage of depending on a subjective slave culture, that is to say on a transfer of the old mass enslavement into the psychological sphere, with the result that, while collective culture was enhanced, individual culture was degraded. Just as the enslavement of the masses was the open wound of the ancient world, so the enslavement of the inferior functions is an ever-bleeding wound in the psyche of modern man. (CW 6:108)

In this psychological version of the master-slave dialectic there is a certain sense of paradox that returns us to the problem of projection. The paradox is that the increased valuation of the inner world is the cause of the material emancipation of the individual. This is due to the projection of interior value onto the object. "Love thy neighbor as thy self" might be the most appropriate expression of this process. The problem is, as Jung points out, that as projection of value takes place on an unconscious level, consciousness of self becomes degraded; in the Christian context the person thinks of himself as a sinner. A multilayered structure of contradictory claims is established within which a major historical force like Christianity must work itself out. This tendency to produce the opposite, the contradictory, brings us back to Gnosticism, which stands as the counter pole in the antique mentality, not only to Christianity, but also to the main philosophical and religious movements of the age upon which the early orthodoxy built.

Before turning to this historical situation, however, one point must be emphasized: Jung's strongly dialectical view of the workings of the psyche results in a reinterpretation of Freud's project within a larger historical framework. Thus Jung not only anticipates the Hegelian reinterpretation of psychoanalysis carried out by Ricoeur, Lacan, and others, but the great power of his theory, at this relatively early stage, shows itself in its ability to account for the emergence of Freud's theory within a larger historical context. In what follows, this must be held in mind, because we will find in Jung's interpretation of Christianity and the emergence of Gnosticism a commentary on his relationship to Freud where the problem is also one of orthodoxy and heresy.

Antinomianism and Interpretation

Christianity and most forms of Gnosticism take Jesus as the normative representation of the religious experience. The religious problem is how the individual comes to interact with that representation. The genius of the orthodox fathers rested in their ability to present an interpretation of the presence of the divine in the world that lent itself to establishing a historically viable community and an attendant institutional structure. The Gnostics, on the other hand, failed in precisely this aspect of their project. This distinction between orthodoxy and Gnosticism reflects, at the philosophical level, the essentially antinomian nature of the heresy that insisted on the radical individuality of the religious experience. Regarding this, Jung writes:

> In Gnosticism we see man's unconscious psychology in full flower, almost perverse in its luxuriance; it contained the very thing that most strongly resisted the *regula fidei*, that Promethean and creative spirit which will bow only to the individual soul and to no collective ruling. Although in crude form, we find in Gnosticism what was lacking in the centuries that followed; a belief in the efficacy of individual revelation and individual knowledge. This belief was rooted in the proud feeling of man's affinity with the gods, subject to no human law, and so overmastering that it may even subdue the gods by the sheer power of Gnosis. (CW 6:409)

What happens in Gnosticism, in other words, is the radical assumption by the individual of the right to interpret his or her own religious experience. In effect, one may grant oneself grace by recourse to individual Gnosis.

In psychological terms this antinomianism takes the form of attributing to an expression of the unconscious one's own interpretation

137

rather than appropriating an interpretation from some outside source of authority, such as the church fathers or Sigmund Freud. By taking this antinomian turn, however, we find that the conflict between heresy and orthodoxy opens up the field of psychoanalysis to the work of phantasy. It is phantasy that makes interpretation possible, and the activity by which phantasy works out its various interpretations is play (CW 6:93). Play is itself a function of the imagination, and the problem with the play of imagination, Jung maintains, is that most people, being in the grip of orthodoxy, are not willing to open up their field of experience to the emergence of the opposites from the unconscious. This "repressed" function is, as in the case of heresy, a threat to consciousness and in most instances it remains safely in the unconscious. Let me point out, however, that what is repressed in Jung's system is the so-called inferior function, which is not at all related to the Freudian vision of repression. Rather, the inferior function represents an alternative interpretation of the experience of reality. It is, rather, the way in which the unconscious is interpreting the experiences that the superior function of consciousness is interpreting in its orthodox manner.

This points us in the direction of Freud's notion of reality-testing and into the midst of the interpretation of psychosis in the sense that psychosis is a profound withdrawal from "reality" to a world of "phantasy." What Jung presents is a model of the psyche where the play of phantasy sets in because the conscious functions cease adequately to interpret the world of experience. Such a failure of the conscious disposition causes a regression of the libido to the unconscious system of meaning, a regression that results in the projection of a new symbolism suited to the interpretation of "reality" in a manner fundamentally different from the previous conscious attitude, but in keeping with the demands of the unconscious (CW 6:314).

In everyday terms, the constellation of a symbol may serve to solve the immediate problem confronting the psyche by providing a much needed counter-interpretation of the situation. But on the historical level the emergence of the symbol is associated with a religious, soteriological function. The sort of crisis that will precipitate the formation of genuine symbol is a spiritual crisis. In the case of Gnosticism, this symbol-forming capacity manifests itself as a continuing counter-tradition within Christianity that works itself out in the form of the Grail legends and later in alchemy. The Grail was of interest to Jung well before 1920, and his commentary on the relationship it held to Gnosticism and orthodoxy provides an example of the workings of phantasy within the counter tradition of a major historical movement. In addition, it gives us an example of how Jung interprets a highly sexual iconography that would otherwise easily come under a classical Freudian interpretation.

Jung contends that one of the most prominent elements of paganism absorbed into Christianity at its inception is the worship of the Great Mother in the person of Mary. The result of this syncretistic assimilation was the suppression, in men, of psychic activity directed toward individual women as the sexual impulse was progressively subordinated to a collective object of worship (CW 6:399). We must also remember that Jung sees in the extraversion of Christianity a reduction of interior images, the self-image, to basically negative characters. This means that the veneration of Mary entails the withdrawal of positive libido from actual women and a regression of libido to infantile images of women as witches or other evil creatures with the attendant projections resulting in the witch hunts (CW6:399). A phantasy, in this case a very negative one, is born out of inappropriately distributed libido. But a relationship exists between the worship of woman and the positive phantasy of the Grail as well. This myth of the holy vessel is, in Jung's opinion, a "relic of Gnosticism" (CW 6:401), that is, of the counter-tradition,[4] and it is the counter-tradition that allows both the spiritualization of the erotic impulse and the constitution of a social order that is not destructive of one half of its participants. The counter-symbol is thus a means of controlling and channeling the activity of libido. This is an extremely complex concept. Within the orthodox tradition, we might say, veneration of the Virgin results in the projection of negative images from the unconscious onto the living woman within the field of consciousness. Within the heterodox or even the heretical tradition the same symbolic quest, as if in objection to the orthodox vision, projects the imagery and produces the social activity associated with courtly love. It is significant that the church consistently objected to the courtly love motif and on several occasions attempted its suppression.

Jung's examination of the Grail legend allows us to expand the notion of the symbol that is so central to his system. Speaking of the Grail, Jung writes:

Experience shows that when the libido is retained, one part of it flows into the spiritualized expression, while the remainder sinks into the unconscious and activates images that correspond to it, in this case the vessel symbol. The symbol lives through the restraint imposed upon certain forms of libido, and in turn serves to restrain these forms. The dissolution of the symbol means a streaming off of libido along the direct path, or at any rate an almost irresistible urge for its direct application. But the living symbol exorcises this danger. A symbol loses its magical or, if you prefer, its redeeming power as soon as its liability to dissolve is recognized. To be effective, a symbol must be by its very nature unassailable. It must be the best possible expression of the prevailing world-view, an unsurpassed container of meaning; it must also be sufficiently remote from comprehension to resist all attempts of the critical intellect to break it down; and finally, its aesthetic form must appeal so convincingly to our feelings that no argument can be raised against it on that score. For a certain time the Grail symbol clearly fulfilled these requirements, and to this fact it owed its vitality, which, as the example of Wagner shows is still not exhausted today, even though our age and our psychology strive unceasingly for its dissolution. (CW 6:401)

Here we find the most penetrating sense of the role of the symbol in channeling libido towards positive encounters with reality. Time, however, plays a central role as Jung associated the symbol with the phenomena we earlier subsumed under the rubric of the boundaries of time and the life cycle of the myth. Historically this vision of the role of the symbol accounts for both the preservation of typified images as expressions of a meaningful experience of the numinous, that is, as timeless expression of the unconscious, and for the investiture of those typifications with new meaning as experience of the numinous is altered by interpretation. The symbol, in other words, is also timely. The structuring of meaning within this frame of time points, as well, to the possibility of a legitimate hermeneutics of mythology and biography by way of the image. This move to the image is, again, at variance with Freud's quest for meaning by way of talk. But, as we have seen, Freud's authority rests on silence and image, thus allowing us to propose that a hermeneutics that seeks to comprehend the significance of Freud's historical achievement must take account of Jung's reconstruction of the nature of meaning in myths by way of the image.

Phantasy and Authority

At this deeper level we confront a situation where the symbol becomes radically self-referential, a definition of the nature of psychoanalysis itself. For Freud is the paradigmatic figure of orthodoxy who establishes a system by developing an interpretation of his own phantasy system that then allows others, indeed, invites others to associate their phantasy systems with his own. Freud's project, in other words, is precisely that of developing, in Jung's words, "an unsurpassed container of meaning" for the modern age. This can only be accomplished, however, by way of the deployment of the elaborate system of authority analyzed in this essay, a system of authority that comes to rest paradoxically in the denial of meaning. Jung rebels against this by taking a profound inward turn, to the unconscious, that results in the creation of an alternative symbolism that, in its attachment to his personal experience, is essentially antinomian. That is to say, Freud cannot invalidate Jung's experience although he may attempt to suppress it, as he and his followers in fact did attempt to do.

Looking at this situation from another point of view, we can see how it is that Freud comes to dominate our conception of the unconscious. The essence of Freud's system is its affinity with the times and the demands for an object suited to the primal projection of modern phantasy. Psychoanalysis is a phantasy system in its very essence, and its power consists in its ability to organize collateral phantasies or projections and to set in motion social functions that serve to reinforce its position. In other words, from the point of view of metabiography developed in this essay and the philosophical view of mythology on which it rests, we are now able to comprehend Freud, and Jung's struggle with him, in a manner that allows us to see that the structure of psychoanalysis, in its most primordial form, represents a prohibition on the formation of alternative systems of interpretation. From the point of view of primal projection, in other words, Freud's psychoanalysis represents the limit of meaning in modernity. This is Freud's great achievement. As we have already seen in chapter six, however, the limit of meaning in psychoanalysis is acted out in silence. Only Jung's escape from Freud's system by way of a return to the unconscious allows us to see beyond the limits of meaning in the modern age.

Eight

Conclusion

Biography and Mythology

We now see how Freud's unwillingness to allow Jung access to his dream, during the ocean passage in 1909, can be interpreted as the representation of authority in psychoanalysis. Freud's mythology gives rise both to an interpretation of the nature of the unconscious and to a course of action intended to vindicate that interpretation by way of the foreclosure of any further investigation of the unconscious as the foundation of meaning. This foreclosure engages psychoanalysis in a contest for dominion over time that is intended to make of Freud's biography something eternal. Biography is thus inextricably linked to mythology, not just in the analysis of a great figure like Leonardo da Vinci, but also in the lives of those who would be psychoanalysts. This essay, therefore, places us in a position to reflect, philosophically, on the grounds for the attribution of meaning in biography. This is the domain of metabiography.

In the first chapter I advanced the idea that claims to authority arise out of systems of interpretation that set themselves the task of bringing worlds into being. At one level, in other words, the interpretations of Freud and Jung are cosmogonic. As such, they perform a mythic role in the psychic economy. Philosophically, they raise the question of how the field of consciousness is constituted. Taking metabiography as the ground for reflection, however, engaged us in linking this constituting project to a course of human action. In the case at hand, the action is embodied in the drama of the confrontation of Jung and Freud, and the drama itself embodies precisely the issues that provide the foundation for their theoretical dispute, which centered on the nature and mechanics of the unconscious.

In this dispute, Jung's argument for primal projection leads to the constitution of a polymorphous world of images. These images become the objects of progressive acts of interpretation, for which change and novelty, both in relations between unconscious and conscious and in the comprehension of the world, are intrinsic capacities. But if the world is constituted for consciousness by repression — the Freudian model — then these polymorphous projections become secondary phenomena, manifest only because of previously repressed contents in the unconscious, and ultimately reducible to a single interpretation. Freud's analysis, therefore, claims an immutable, timeless nature for repression where the same repressions occur, repeatedly, throughout history. Hence the argument concerning the central role of time in the structure of authority made in chapters six and seven. In the case of Jung, on the other hand, the primal projection — for which repression is secondary — establishes a world that consciousness in effect "reads" as it progresses through time (chapter seven). In 1912, therefore, Jung could view an event, such as the star of Bethlehem, as a primal "cosmic" projection. That is, it was a primary object of psychic attention that organized consciousness and the comprehension of time and action during a particular historical period. The psycho-religious significance of this event eventually exhausts itself, however, through the process of interpretation. Thus primal projections are not unchanging in the way primal repression is.

I have argued that Freud's authority, seen in terms of a prohibition on the alteration of the primal image and thus as a prohibition on change itself, is contingent on the assertion of the primacy of repression. But that assertion itself rests on the mythology of the primal killing first proposed in *Totem and Taboo*.

Primordially, Freud's authority must turn in on its foundation and vindicate this logic of repression. Such a turning requires that Freud vindicate the logic of the primal killing. This leads us to conclude that authority itself ultimately comes to rest, for Freud, in the replacement of the natural inevitability of death with the necessity of killing. With this we confront an inversion of the problem of death and authority outlined in Hegel and find Freud offering a solution to the threat to authority posed by the fact that death is an assertion of the primacy of the natural order over the civil order. The myth of the primal killing asserts that just the opposite state of affairs is the case in that the only psychically important death is the killing of the father, which is not a death at all in the sense provided by the natural order. By way of the development of this mythology, Freud displaces the primordial, existential encounter with death into the world of culture, of civilization, and thereby gives to the institutions of authority the prerogative of judging all subsequent interpretations of existence. To put it another way, the power of the myth of the primal killing rests in the claim that the origins of the systems of the psyche — unconscious, preconscious, conscious or later the id, ego, and super-ego — and the origins of the project of culture, coincide with this primal event, and that all subsequent acts of human enterprise look back at this event to establish their true meaning.

Seen from the metabiographical point of view, this assertion of the primacy of killing is the constitutive moment in the definition of a possible system of self-understanding. Both death as killing and retrospective temporal interpretation are thus seen to satisfy the requirements of the question *de jure* that introduced the concept of metabiography. Oedipus, in the Freudian interpretation, then becomes the mythic representation of biography. The problem with this solution to the metabiographical problematic, however, is that the mythology of the primal killing can only be vindicated by means of a hermeneutics of suspicion that engages Freud in a struggle for authority over interpretation that breaks down in that moment when access to the biography of Freud becomes necessary. Then, because of the breakdown of Freud's authority, new metabiographical possibilities become evident as access to the ultimate object of psychoanalytic inquiry, the unconscious itself, becomes a possibility for Jung.

Jung's Struggle with Freud

Jung encountered the authority of Freud's system by way of Freud's metabiographical categories and deployed an alternative mythology that reordered his actions within the frame of time in such a way that he escaped from Freud's authority and gained entrance to the unconscious, at first in a manner that he interpreted as a psychosis. This alternative is at the heart of Jung's struggle with Freud.

Jung's Gnostic mythology seeks the projection of an imagery that, through successive acts of interpretation, will allow him to overcome Freud's projected mythology of the primal killing. In chapter two, I demonstrated we do have grounds to validate Jung's childhood experiences as found in his autobiography. The point of this validation was the introduction into the dialogue with Freud of a proto-Gnostic metaphor from Jung's childhood. In other words, there is evidence that, from an early point in his life, Jung had experiences that conformed in some sense to a Gnostic myth cycle. These included, it will be recalled, the notion of dual personality and particularly the dual or primal mother; the absence of the father from the network of primal figures; and the experience of the specific dispensation of grace from a god who is beyond the representative of the church. But the crucial point for understanding the role this Gnostic myth plays in Jung's project of escaping from the authority of Freud is the emphasis on the feminine in the constitution of meaning. The claim that the unconscious itself occupies the place of the mother in the Oedipal struggle of the two protagonists is vital to the argument and to an understanding of the historical world for which the unconscious has become thematic. Collaterally, the relative insignificance of the father in Jung's Gnostic myth makes the killing of the father an equally insignificant act while the mother emerges as the central figure.

It is important at this point to recall the precise understanding of the incest prohibition, developed by recourse to Jung (chapters five and seven). Freud's myth of the primal killing establishes a prohibition on the return to the mother. This means that the son, in the person of Jung, is prohibited by Freud from undertaking his own investigation and interpretation of the unconscious. But we must also note that this entire negative system of values rests on the father as legislator. Now if, as in the Gnostic cosmology to which Jung turns, the feminine Sophia is the most proximate source of man's being, then we have the key to Jung's Gnostic metaphor as it enters into his mature thought. It is essentially tied up with rejection of Freud's astonishingly limited interpretation of incest.

Image and Time

A dogmatic system must assert its power to achieve transhistorically valid interpretations. This is the argument of Chapter 6, where Freud's assertion of the timelessness of the unconscious is examined. Only the claim of the unchanging nature of the unconscious gives Freud grounds to set up the Oedipus drama as the single valid interpretation of unconscious experience. Only in this way can he claim that every person who comes into the world must face this problem, and then make the attendant claim that the Oedipal situation is the foundation of culture.

The element of action in this argument, which brings us into contact with mythology, is Freud's acting out of a primal confrontation and killing at strategic moments in his relations with close followers. Just as in Jung's analysis of the somnambulist, where I argued that the true telos of the event was the emergence of the psychologist, C. G. Jung, not at all (or, at least, only incidentally) the maturation of his cousin Helene, so in the fainting spells we have what is termed the presentation of an image for the psyche — in this case an image of the killing of the father — which seeks to organize the psychic activity of the observer. This point must be clear. The occult experiences of the seance open a space for interpretation by alienating the person from commonsense experience. The event displaces the person. But the occult phenomenon also provides an image that allows interpretation to take place.

Thus both cases, Helene's seances and Freud's fainting, an action is inextricably tied up with the presentation of a thought. In the first case Jung's involvement leads to a particular sense of the psyche that allows him to embark on his career as a psychologist. In the case of Freud's fainting spells the orthodox interpretation would lead Jung to become a Freudian psychoanalyst. His decision, however, is to reject the image presented by Freud and seek his own interpretation of the unconscious.

Thought, Action, and Symbol

I charge Freud with presenting an image. This means that Freud acts in a manner that is totally contrary to his quest for the linguistic structure behind the image. But in his desire to die and thereby absolutize his claims to authority, Freud had to reject the honest talk of analysis, just as in 1909 he refused to continue his analysis with Jung for fear of his authority. The purpose of this foreclosure was to cause Jung to view an image of himself in the pose of killing the primal father. According to Jung's theory of projection, this would result in the constitution of a primal image in the unconscious. The Oedipus complex would then be vindicated by image and projection rather than by word and repression. Thus we come to the primacy of the image from within Freud's system by an examination of the existential component and, in particular, of the vivid acting out of the essential dogmatic myth.

Psychosis: The Quest for Meaning

This image of the killing is the hinge on which Jung's encounter with the unconscious turns. In essence, Freud tempts Jung in the sense that he presents a possible interpretation of the numinous world of the unconscious intended to bind the younger man to him. That is to say, Freud presents to Jung the image of a complete world of meaning in his acting out of the primal killing. Jung, however, rejects this image as the only one suitable for the interpretation of the numinous. This necessitates that he relinquish the immediate possibility of secure interpretation, provided by Freud's system, and step into the void, acting out the mythology of self-sacrifice. As Jung remarked in 1925, he did not have his own myth system ready in any articulate form to fill the void and thus came to the near-psychotic loss of reality. This journey through the void of meaninglessness ended with the writing of the *Seven Sermons*. The significance of the *Sermons* now becomes clear. They mark the concrete constitution of an interpretation suited to a previously inarticulate lived experience of the numinous that Jung had refused to subordinate to Freud's interpretation. The development and articulation of the Gnostic myth, in the years following the break with Freud, is thus a search for a mythology that can at least reduce to proper dimensions, if not actually overcome, the myth of the primal killing. But we must remember that Freud's myth of the killing is extremely powerful. It is a genuine interpretation of the numinous, and therefore Jung's search for an alternative interpretation is not simply a casual, intellectual game of casting about for a more pleasing description of sexual impulses. It is, in fact, an attempt to establish an alternative universe of understanding and action.

The Individual Image

Here we must recall the argument of chapter four, where I pointed to Ricoeur's reservations concerning the constitution of meaning in the midst of the system of force, deployed by Freud, that seems ultimately intended to prevent the emergence of new meanings. Tied to the idea of the boundaries of time, this dependence on force, directed against the primacy of the image, results in Freud's domination of time. But, strangely, this places a severe strain on Freud himself, because Freud's Egyptian myth continues to work itself out in his own psychic world in terms of a historically evolving image. We are, for example, constantly confronted in Freud's writings with the inconclusive, highly impressionistic meditations on the Egyptian Moses as an image. There is the statue of Moses and the history of Moses but there is no Moses complex about which we could talk in therapy. His study, "The Moses of Michelangelo," which he first published anonymously, is a case in point. Here Freud "confesses" his sense of inadequacy before the polymorphous meanings of the great image. The network of neurosis which Freud spun round the figure of Moses has been addressed by many commentators (see particularly Rice 1990 and Yerushalmi 1991), but I want to claim that Freud's obsession with the Egyptian goes far beyond the merely neurotic.

What is the meaning of Freud's rejection of the image in favor of the word? I take it that if the image is given primacy several things happen that tend to undermine the very possibility of authority in psychoanalysis. At its most elementary level the primacy of the image disturbs the essential relationship to the analyst as it is found in Freudian theory. To turn to the image is to turn away from discourse. The classic representative of this turn was, again, Brother Klaus who, as a hermit, turned away from the community, that is, away from a world of discourse, to a world of images which served to organize his unique personal experience. Thereafter, the community, in the form of the church with its deep interest in authority, took steps to reclaim the images of the saint for its own purposes within its system of discourse. In the actions of the hermit, we begin to approach the foundations of the antinomian impulse in the assault of the image on the discursive articulation of a dogmatic system.

Just as Brother Klaus turned to the image of the Trinity, so the image of the Egyptian Moses haunts Freud, and Jung turns to the Gnostics. But the Gnostics present a curious variation on the theme of the image, for they actively encourage the formation of highly individualized interpretations precisely because of their avowed antinomianism. Ultimately they promote a radical individualism of the image. The point, therefore, is that Jung selects an image system to organize his experiences that is fundamentally at variance with the program of Freud's mythology. But Freud had validated just this process of individual image selection in his presentation of the Egyptian motif in the study of Leonardo, which prompted Jung to assert the unity of biography and mythology in the first place. Thus Freud collaborates in the formation of a counter-myth to that myth upon which psychoanalysis is supposed to rest, the myth of Oedipus. This returns us to the question of what status the Oedipus complex actually enjoys in the authority structure of Freud's project.

Oedipus

From Jung's point of view, Freud's interpretation of the Oedipus myth unquestionably defines one range of possible self-understanding available to the modern age. This is why Jung never argued that Freud was simply incorrect in his theory of the psyche. To the contrary, Freud is revealed by Jung to have been immensely successful in setting up a system of interpretation. The issue, however, is that Freud's objective was not simply to establish one successful system of interpretation among others. Rather, Freud was concerned to establish the transhistorical and unchanging nature of the Oedipus complex as the foundation of the "true" system of interpretation. Because of the role of the killing of the father in this myth system, however, Freud had to assert the primacy of repression. This leads to the conclusion that in Freud's hands Oedipus and the taboo against incest close off access to the unconscious. In other words, once the unconscious is interpreted by recourse to Freud's reading of this myth, it is possible to prevent any other interpretation from taking place. This is the goal and function of a dogmatic symbol: that it provide a powerful interpretation of a numinous experience and that it prevent any further interpretations.

Jung's alternative, we have seen, is to claim primacy for projection, as opposed to repression, as the constituting mechanism of the psyche. The analysis of projection shows us that time is the essential problem for any system of interpretation in which a mythology is a constitutive element. This means that any system of authority, built on a foundation of interpretation directed toward a mythology, is itself structured in relation to the problem of time, which is now seen as a desire for the domination of time itself. We also see that projection gives to the Oedipus drama a multitude of possible interpretations because of projection's prospective orientation and its capacity to excite ever new acts of interpretation. Projection — with all its connotations of the setting of a project — opens the unconscious toward the future. In the end, this is the answer to the problem of authority in psychoanalysis and, perhaps, in those domains of political thinking for which psychoanalysis has become thematic. Repression becomes the central problem for understanding authority insofar as the analytic of repression is itself the ground of repressive, authoritarian systems. To put it another way, the analytic of repression, as practiced by Freud and those political thinkers who appropriate him, results in a closure of interpretation and a loss of both past and future. Interpretation has no past because of its claim to be the first expression of true historical understanding. And it has no future because its claim to legitimacy must ultimately reject novelty and innovation. The irony of this conclusion, that an emancipatory project leads to the complete closure of temporal understanding, opens the space of thinking for a reassessment of the place and function of interpretation in understanding human association.

Notes

Chapter One

1. In 1957 John M. Billinsky, a professor at Andover Newton Seminary, had a conversation with Jung where the topic of this dream came up. Billinsky reports that Jung gave the following account of his first meetings with Freud and of the dream in question:

"I first met Freud in 1906. I talked with him for hours and hours. Although I was very much impressed with him, I was also somewhat confused. He was very serious about his theory of sex, but somehow the more he spoke about it, the more doubts there were in my mind. Indeed, some things did not become clear to me until after our friendship ended.

"In 1907 I wrote Freud a letter telling him that I was going to visit him in Vienna. When I arrived in Vienna with my young and happy wife, Freud came to see us at the hotel and brought some flowers for my wife. He was trying to be very considerate and at one point he said to me, 'I am sorry that I can give you no real hospitality; I have nothing at home but an elderly wife.' When my wife heard him say that, she looked perturbed and embarrassed.

"At Freud's home that evening, during dinner, I tried to talk to Freud and his wife about psychoanalysis and Freud's activities, but I soon discovered that Mrs. Freud knew absolutely nothing about what Freud was doing. It was very obvious that there was a very superficial relationship between Freud and his wife.

"Soon I met Freud's wife's younger sister. She was very good-looking and she not only knew enough about psychoanalysis but also about everything that Freud was doing. When, a few days later, I tried visiting Freud's laboratory, Freud's sister-in-law asked me if she could talk with me. She was very much bothered by her relationship with Freud and felt guilty about it. From her I learned that Freud was in love with her and that their relationship was indeed very intimate. It was a shocking discovery to me, and even now I can recall the agony I felt at the time.

"Two years later Freud and I were invited to Clark University in Worcester, and we were together every day for some seven weeks. From the very beginning of our trip we started to analyze each other's dreams. Freud had some dreams that bothered him very much. The dreams were about the triangle—Freud, his wife, and wife's younger sister. Freud had no idea that I knew about the triangle and his intimate relationship with his sister-in-law. And so, when Freud told me about the dream in which his wife and her sister played important parts, I asked Freud to tell me some of his personal associations with the dream. He looked at me with bitterness and said, 'I could tell you more, but I cannot risk my authority.' That of course, finished my attempt to deal with his dreams. During the trip Freud developed severe neuroses, and I had to do limited analysis with him. He had psychosomatic troubles and had difficulties in controlling his bladder. I suggested to Freud that he should have complete analysis, but he rebelled against such an idea because he would have had to deal with problems that were closely related to his theories. If Freud would have tried to understand consciously the triangle, he would have been much, much better off." (Billinsky 1969:42)

Numerous writers have referred to rumors of Freud's involvement with his sister-in-law and to the Billinsky interview. Until recently there has been a nearly universal tendency to discount the imputation of a sexual relationship between Freud and Minna Bernays. Kaufmann, in fact, records, concerning the Billinsky account, that "those who were perhaps closest to Jung insisted that, according to what Jung had said more than once about Freud's character, this [the Billinsky account] was absolutely wrong" (Kaufmann 1980:379). This assertion is not borne out by Jung's close associate, Professor Carl A. Meier, however. In an interview for the C. G. Jung Biographical Archive at Harvard he corroborates Billinsky's account and is only upset that Jung would confide in someone he knew only slightly (C. G. Jung Biographical Archive, Box 6:p54).

In 1981, Peter Swales reported investigations into Freud's relationship with Minna Bernays that point far more conclusively to a sexual affair and, possibly, to her having become pregnant, with a subsequent abortion in Italy (*The New York Times*, November 1981).

Based on the evidence I have seen it appears certain that Freud was deeply involved with Minna Bernays and that Jung's claim that this played a role in the shipboard dream is accurate. As will be evident as my argument progresses, however, this is not the decisive aspect of the conflict between the two men although Freud's indulgence in a form of incest, as well as Jung's affairs with Sabina Spielrein and Toni Wolff, can be taken as icons of the deep structure of their struggle.

2. This has been discussed with considerable insight by Stepansky and I do not intend to repeat his investigations here, although I recommend his article to anyone interested in this phase of the history of psychoanalysis (Stepansky 1976).

3. A notable exception to this is Liliane Frey-Rohn's moderate and even-handed study, *From Freud to Jung* which I recommend highly. I also recommend the recent study by Homans, *Jung in Context: Modernity and the Making of a Psychology* which builds an insightful argument on the association of the two men. Homans gives us a striking picture of Jung and the narcissistic problem in the modern world. He is also attentive to the central role, in Jung, of projection and phantasy. Similarly, Robert S. Steele's *Freud and Jung: Conflicts of Interpretation*, which appeared as this book was going to press, marks a further deepening of interest in the history and systematic impact of the relationship between the two men.

Chapter Two

1. It is worth noting that this passage also reflects Jung's notion that dreams are not simply discrete elements in the psychic economy, but can make up extended patterns of interconnected and evolving meanings. This leads to the conception of transformation which Jung worked out at a later date (see chapter six, part II).

Chapter Three

1. One would do well to investigate Schur's discussion of Freud's obsession with the death of his brother in light of his apparent need to place this myth of the brothers within the strictest biological confines. Although I will not take up the issue in this study, I would venture to say that Freud himself is repressing or censoring this painful episode in his own past.

2. It is interesting to note that in 1924 Freud comments in an addendum to *Three Essays* that Otto Rank "has traced attachment to the mother back to the intra-uterine period and has thus indicated the biological foundation of the Oedipus complex" (SE VII:226). Shortly thereafter Freud expelled Rank from the inner circle of psychoanalysis.

3. Jung refers to Freud's Schreber study, SE XII:75.

4. In his autobiography Jung is eloquent on the nature of Freud's dogmatic view of sexuality:

> Freud, who had always made much of his irreligiosity, had now constructed a dogma; or rather, in the place of a jealous God whom he had lost, he had substituted another compelling image, that of sexuality. It was no less insistent, exacting, domineering, threatening, and morally ambivalent than the original one. Just as the physically stronger agency is given "divine" or "daemonic" attributes, so the "sexual libido" took over the role of a *deus absconditus*, a hidden or concealed god. (MDR 151)

5. Eckermann records the following remark by Goethe on this point: "I would have thought, said Goethe, that the love between sister and sister would be purer and less sexual. As if it were not a matter of record, that there are uncounted known and unknown cases in which the most sensual affection existed between brother and sister" (*Gesprache mit Goethe*, March 28, 1827, my translation). It also seems that there were traditions of the Antigone myth, not used by Sophocles, in which Antigone and Polyneices were not only siblings, but were also married to each other. It may also be, if Immanuel Velikovsky is correct (Velikovsky, *Oedipus and Akhnaton*) that a tradition existed where Antigone became her father's consort. This would not be an exaggeration of the myth for, as I will show, it becomes extremely complex even in its Sophoclean incarnation (chapters five and seven). I wish to thank Kristin Pfefferkorn for the information in this note.

6. The exact comment which Jones records is "Then [i.e., in *The Interpretation of Dreams*] I described the wish to kill one's father, and now I have been describing the actual killing; after all it is a big step from a wish to a deed."

Chapter Four

1. It is also important to note that Freud's conception of the unconscious changed dramatically with time. In 1920, with the postulation of the second topography (id, ego, superego), each level of mental activity was invested with an unconscious component. I will not address this later development in detail since my concern is with the origins of the unconscious no matter what its form.

2. More properly, both in terms of translation and for the preservation of the economic metaphor intended, Freud's term *Besetzung*, here translated as cathexis in the Standard Edition, would be better translated as "investment" while "anti-cathexis" would correspond to "withdrawal."

3. Schur has given an excellent analysis of Freud's fainting fits from within the psychoanalytic tradition and with extensive reference to correspondence of the time which also attempts to analyze the events. Jones, of course, refers to the problem but does not offer as complete an analysis as Schur who, I want to emphasize, sees the problem in the context of Freud's obsession with death. There is also the insightful discussion by Velikovsky of the unacknowledged relationship between Abraham's paper and Freud's *Moses and Monotheism*. Velikovsky makes the point that in *Moses*, Akhnaton appears singularly well adjusted while Abraham had portrayed him as a serious neurotic (Velikovsky 1960:200). The implications of this shift are many. I would simply note that Freud seems to have come around to Jung's point of view in the last analysis of this Oedipal situation.

4. This would also be the case where castration is concerned. In the great myth cycles one typically finds the motif of castration of the father by the son. This flies in the face of Freud's notion of castration where it is the child that fears he will be castrated by the father.

Chapter Five

I. *Transformations* was revised in 1950 to conform to views Jung had developed since its original publication in 1912. To a great degree the revisions can already be found in Jung's unpublished seminars of the 1920's and 1930's. In many respects this revision, now titled *Symbols of Transformation*, is the same as the original. Jung introduced the vocabulary of the archetypes, which he had not used prior to 1919, and made some other revisions which are not critical to the argument. Due to my concern for the actual confrontation between Freud and Jung, however, I have consulted the original text while collating it to the translation found in the *Collected Works*. Some passages added to the 1950 edition are cited in footnotes for the light they throw on Jung's position.

2. Jung's comment in 1925 was: "I had written a book about the hero, I had explained the myths of past peoples, but what about my own myth? I had to admit I had none; I knew theirs but none of my own, nor did anyone else have one today."

3. Our understanding of *Transformations* has been significantly altered due to the investigations of Sonu Shamdasani (1990) who has discovered that Frank Miller took on the fabrication of her phantasies while in sound mental condition. These facts, however, do not materially alter the argument in this essay.

4. In a passage added to the revised version of *Transformations* Jung addresses these issues:

> Scenting the dangers in this situation, religious and conventional morality joins forces with Freudian theory in consistently devaluing the regression and its ostensible goal—reversion to infantilism—as "infantile sexuality," "incest," "uterine fantasy," etc. . . . What is more, moral condemnation seizes upon the regressive tendency and tries by every trick of devaluation to prevent this sacrilegious return to the mother. . . But anything that exceeds the bounds of a man's personal consciousness remains unconscious and therefore appears in projection; that is to say, the semi-animal psyche with its regressive demands against which he struggles so desperately is attributed to the mother, and the defense against it is seen in the father. Projection, however, is never a cure; it prevents the conflict only on the surface, while deeper down it creates a neurosis which allows him to escape into illness. (CW 5:507)

This passage, although added later, highlights a crucial point in the interpretation of the Freud-Jung controversy. For what Jung is arguing is that the authority attributed to the father in the prohibition of incest is in fact a projection of the fear experienced by the individual's own encounter with incest, with the desire to regress to the unconscious in the form of the mother. In other words, any injunction on the part of the father is a second-ary phenomenon, as Jung had claimed in his letters to Freud.

5. This is particularly the case in the second half of life — the period when Jung claims his psychology is most appropriate. In the 1950 edition Jung wrote:

> What must be regarded as regression in a young person — feminization of the man (partial identity with the mother) and mascu-linization of the woman (partial identity with the father) — acquires a different meaning in the second half of life. The assimilation of the contrasexual tendencies then becomes a task that must be fulfilled in order to keep the libido in a state of progression, the task consists in integrating the unconscious, in bringing together "conscious" and "unconscious." (CW 5:459)

It is worth pointing out that both male and female personalities have the project before them of assimilating the contrasexual, i.e. the task of becom-ing the hero. It would be interesting to examine the figure of Antigone in this light.

6. Indeed, in a continuation of the passage added to the text in 1950, cited in note 4, Jung argues that it is the function of therapy itself to aid in effecting the conquest of the restrictive force, which prohibits entry to the unconscious:

> therapy must support the regression, and continue to do so until the "prenatal" stage is reached. It must be remembered that the "mother" is really an imago, a psychic image merely, which has in it a number of different but very important unconscious contents. The "mother," as the first incarnation of the anima archetype, personifies in fact the whole unconscious. Hence the regression leads back only apparently to the mother; in reality she is the gateway into the unconscious, into the "realm of the Mother." Whoever sets foot in the realm submits his conscious ego-personality to the controlling influence of the uncon-scious, or if he feels that he has got caught by mistake, or that some-body has tricked him into it, he will defend himself desperately, though his resistance will not turn out to his advantage. For regression, if left undisturbed, does not stop at the "mother" but goes back beyond her to the prenatal realm of the "Eternal Feminine," to the immortal world of archetypal possibilities where, "thronged round with images of all creation," slumbers the "divine child," patiently

awaiting his conscious realization. This son is the germ of wholeness and he is characterized as such by his specific symbols. (CW 5:508)

This remarkable passage carries us a great distance in understanding the nature of the conflict between Freud and Jung, not to mention the general understanding of Jung's conception of the psyche. The hero, the divine child, is the product of the incestuous turn. In this sense the divine child is self-generated, and it is at this point that he replaces the father. In the original 1912 text, Jung had pointed to this idea with the words, "the hero is his own father and his own begetter" (CW 5:516).

Chapter Six

1. In September 1913, Lou Andreas-Salome wrote "Freud always empha- sizes that by 'timeless' he means unabreacted and no more" (Andreas- Salome 1964:170). This claim is not borne out by Freud's own published claims. True, repressed experiences may be said to remain unchanged until abreaction takes place, but Freud's real concern was to exempt the processes and not simply the specific contents of the unconscious from alteration over time. To a degree, of course, these are synonymous since the processes largely determine the content of the unconscious (see above chapter four).

2. Cf. *Moses and Monotheism*, section II, part 4 (SE XXIII: II lff.). Also chapter four above.

3. This aspect of schizophrenia has been explored most thoroughly by the existential psychologists such as Jaspers and Minkowski.

4. Harries 1970:140, comments on Marcuse's interpretation of Nietzsche.

Chapter Seven

1. This note was somewhat altered in the 1950 revision and I therefore cite the English translation of 1916.

2. The notion of the archetype is difficult to work out with any degree of precision. Like Freud's description of the structure of the unconscious, the theory of the archetypes undergoes constant revision throughout Jung's later writings. Since the theory was not even articulated until near the end of the period I am dealing with in this essay, I will not take it up at this time beyond making the observation that the development of a personal myth rests, ultimately, on the emergence of images appropriate to each individ- ual's encounter with the archetypes. This is the process Jung went through in his encounter with the unconscious and, given the argument of this essay concerning Freud's mythology, we can at least hypothesize a similar experi- ence in his life.

3. The interested reader should consult Jung's autobiography for the complete text of the sermons.

4. Jung undoubtedly had Jessie L. Weston's influential book, *From Ritual to Romance*, in his possession by 1921. Weston, of course, argues for a Gnostic origin to the Grail legend based on G. R. S. Mead's rendering of a Naasene text. Interestingly, Weston does not consider Wolfram's Grail to be Gnostic in origin while the Kahanes make just this connection to Hermetic Gnosticism in their study, *The Krater and the Grail: Hermetic Sources of the Parzival.*

Bibliography

Andreas-Salome, Lou. *The Freud Journal of Lou Andreas-Salome*, trans. S. A. Leavy. New York: Basic Books, 1964.

Bachofen, Johann Jakob. *Myth, Religion and Mother Right: Selected Writings of J. J. Bachofen*, trans. R. Manheim. Princeton, N.J.: Bollingen Series 84, Princeton University Press, 1967.

Billinsky, John M. "Jung and Freud (The End of a Romance)." *Andover Newton Quarterly*, November 1969, pp. 39–43.

Bleuler, Eugen. *Dementia Precox or the Group of Schizophrenias*, trans. J. Zinkin. New York: International Universities Press, 1950.

Boas, George, trans. *The Hieroglyphics of Horapollo*. New York: Bollingen Series 23, Pantheon Books, 1950.

Campbell, Joseph, ed. *Papers from the Eranos Yearbooks*, 6 vols. Princeton, N.J.: Bollingen Series 100, Princeton University Press, 1954 and later.

Dobbs, Betty Jo Teeter. *The Foundations of Newton's Alchemy or "The Hunting of the Greene Lyon."* Cambridge: Cambridge University Press, 1975.

Eckermann, Johann Peter. *Gesprache mit Goethe in den letzten Jahren seines Lebens*, hrsg. L. Geiger. Leipzig: Max Hesse Verlag, 1902.

Freud, Sigmund. *The Standard Edition of the Complete Psychological Works of Sigmund Freud*, James Strachey, ed., in collaboration with Anna Freud, assisted by Alix Strachey and Alan Tyson, 24 vols. London: The Hogarth Press, 1953–1964.

Frey-Rohn, Liliane. *From Freud to Jung: A Comparative Study of the Psychology of the Unconscious*, trans. F. and E. Engreen. New York: G. P. Putnam, 1974.

Guthrie, W. K. C. *The Greeks and Their Gods*. Boston: Beacon Press, 1955.

Haardt, Robert. "Gnosis" in Karl Rahner, ed., *Sacramentum Mundi*, vol. 2, pp. 374–379. New York: Herder and Herder, 1968.

Harries, Karsten. "Death and Utopia: Towards a Critique of the Ethics of Satisfaction," *Research in Phenomenology* (1977), pp. 138–152.

Hegel, G. W. F. *Phenomenology of Spirit*, trans. A. V. Miller. Oxford: Clarendon Press, 1977.

Hegel, G. W. F. *Philosophy of Right*, trans. T. M. Knox. London: Oxford University Press, 1976.

Hillman, James. "Notes on C. G. Jung's Medium, by Stefanie Zumstein-Preiswerk," *Spring* (1976), pp. 123–137.

Homans, Peter. *Jung in Context: Modernity and the Making of a Psychology*. Chicago: The University of Chicago Press, 1979.

Jonas, Hans. *The Gnostic Religion: The Message of the Alien God and the Beginnings of Christianity*. Boston: Beacon Press, 1963.

Jones, Ernest. *The Life and Works of Sigmund Freud*, 3 vols. New York: Basic Books, 1957.

Jung, C. G. *Analytical Psychology: Notes of the Seminar Given in 1925 by C. G. Jung*. Princeton, N.J.: Bollingen Series 99, Princeton University Press, 1989.

Jung, C. G. *The Collected Works of C. G. Jung*, 20 vols. Editors: Sir Herbert Read, Michael Fordham, Gerhard Adler; William McGuire, Executive Editor. Trans. R. F. C. Hull (except vol. 2). Princeton, N.J.: Princeton University Press, 1953–1979.

Jung, C. G. *Memories, Dreams Reflection*. Recorded and edited by A. Jaffe, trans. R. and C. Winston. New York: Pantheon Books, 1963.

Jung, C. G. *Psychology of the Unconscious: A Study of the Transformations and Symbols of the Libido*, trans. B. M. Hinkle. New York: Moffat, Yard, and Co., 1916

Kahane, Henry and Renee with A. Pietrangeli. *The Krater and the Grail: Hermetic Sources of the Parzival*. Urbana, Il.: University of Illinois Press, 1965.

Kaufmann, Walter. *Discovering the Mind: Freud Versus Adler and Jung*. New York: McGraw-Hill, 1980.

Kerenyi, Carl. *Eleusis: Archetypal Image of the Mother and Daughter*, trans. R. Manheim. New York: Schocken Books, 1977.

Kerenyi, Carl. *The Heroes of the Greeks*. London: Thames and Hudson, 1978.

Lacan, Jacques. *The Language of the Self: The Function of Language in Psychoanalysis*, trans. and commentary by A. Wilden. New York: Dell, 1968.

Laplance, J. and J. B. Pontalis. *The Language of Psycho-analysis*, trans. D. Nicholson-Smith. New York: W. W. Norton, 1973.

Lenoir, Timothy. *The Strategy of Life: Teleology and Mechanics in Nineteenth-Century German Biology*. Chicago: The University of Chicago Press, 1982.

McGuire, William, ed. *The Freud/Jung Letters: The Correspondence Between Sigmund Freud and C. G. Jung*. Trans. R. Manheim and R. F. C. Hull. Princeton, N.J.: Bollingen Series 94, Princeton University Press, 1974.

McGuire, William and R. F. C. Hull, eds. *C. G. Jung Speaking: Interviews and Encounters*. Princeton, N.J.: Bollingen Series 98, Princeton University Press, 1977.

Maidenbaum, Aryeh, and Stephen A. Martin, eds. *Lingering Shadows: Jungians, Freudians and Anti-Semitism*. Boston: Shambhala, 1991.

Marcuse, Herbert. *Eros and Civilization: A Philosophical Inquiry into Freud*. Boston: Beacon Press, 1966.

Nietzsche, Friedrich. *Thus Spoke Zarathustra*, trans. W. Kaufmann. New York: Penguin Books, 1967.

Nietzsche, Friedrich. *The Will to Power*, trans. W. Kaufmann and R. J. Hollingdale. New York: Vintage Books, 1967.

Nunberg, Herman and Ernst Federn, eds. *Minutes of the Vienna Psychoanalytic Society, Volume III: 1910–1911*, trans. M. Nunberg. New York: International Universities Press, 1970.

Rice, Emanuel. *Freud and Moses: The Long Journey Home*. Albany: The State University of New York Press, 1990.

Ricoeur, Paul. *Freud and Philosophy: An Essay on Interpretation*, trans. D. Savage. New Haven, Conn.: Yale University Press, 1970.

Ricoeur, Paul. *The Symbolism of Evil*, trans. E. Buchanan. Boston: Beacon Press, 1967.

Rieff, Philip. *Freud: The Mind of the Moralist*. Chicago: The University of Chicago Press, 1979.

Rieff, Philip. *The Triumph of the Therapeutic: Uses of Faith After Freud*. New York: Harper and Row, 1968.

Robert, Marthe. *From Oedipus to Moses: Freud's Jewish Identity*, trans. R. Manheim. Garden City, N.Y.: Anchor Books, 1976.

Schur, Max. *Freud: Living and Dying*. New York: International Universities Press, 1972.

Shamdasani, Sonu. "A Woman Called Frank." *Spring* 50 (1990), pp. 26–56.

Steele, Robert S. *Freud and Jung: Conflicts of Interpretation*. London: Routledge and Kegan Paul, 1982.

Stepansky, Paul E. "The Empiricist as Rebel: Jung, Freud, and Burdens of Discipleship," *Journal of the History of the Behavioral Sciences* 12 (1976), pp. 216–239.

Velikovsky, Immanuel. *Oedipus and Akhnaton: Myth and History*. New York: Doubleday, 1960.

Yates, Frances. *Giordano Bruno and the Hermetic Tradition*. London: Routledge and Kegan Paul, 1964.

Yates, Frances. *The Rosicrucian Enlightenment*. Boulder: Shambala, 1978.

Yerushalmi, Yosef Hayim. *Freud's Moses: Judaism Terminable and Interminable*. New Haven, Conn.: Yale University Press, 1991.

Index